NORSE
MYTHOLOGY

THE MYTHOLOGY LIBRARY
NORSE MYTHOLOGY

THE MYTHS AND LEGENDS OF THE NORDIC GODS

ARTHUR COTTERELL

ULTIMATE
EDITIONS

This edition published in the UK in 1997 by
ULTIMATE EDITIONS

© 1997 ANNESS PUBLISHING LIMITED

ULTIMATE EDITIONS
is an imprint of Anness Publishing Limited
Hermes House, 88-89 Blackfriars Road
London SE1 8HA

This edition distributed in Canada by
Raincoast Books Distribution Limited

ISBN 1 86035 262 6

Publisher: Joanna Lorenz
Editorial Manager: Helen Sudell
Project Editor: Belinda Wilkinson
Designer: Nigel Soper, Millions Design
Illustrators: James Alexander, Nick Beale,
Glenn Steward

Previously published as part of a larger
compendium, *The Encyclopedia of Mythology*

Printed in Singapore by Star Standard Industries Pte. Ltd.
10 9 8 7 6 5 4 3 2 1

Page One: Woodcarving, 12th Century
Frontispiece: *The Forging of the Sampo* by A.
Gallen-Kallela
This page: *Thos in the Boat of Hymir* by F. Fusell

Author's Note
The entries in this encyclopedia are all
listed alphabetically. Where more than one
name exists for a character the entry is
listed under the name used in the original
country of origin for that particular myth.
Names in italic capital letters indicate that
that name has an individual entry. Special
feature spreads examine specific
mythological themes in more detail. If a
character is included in a special feature
spread it is noted at the end of their
individual entry.

CONTENTS

NORSE
MYTHOLOGY

INTRODUCTION

THE MYTHOLOGY OF NORTHERN AND eastern Europe is essentially that of two main groups, peoples of Germanic and of Slavic descent. Today the former group includes Germans, Dutch, Danes, Swedes, Norwegians, Icelanders, English, and any of their extraction, while the Slavs are made up of Russians, Serbs, Croats, Bulgarians, Rumanians, Slovacs and Poles. Other peoples have also contributed to the mythological tradition of the region, such as the inhabitants of the Baltic shore: the Prussians, Lithuanians and Letts. Further north there are contributions from the Finns and the Lapps of Sweden and Norway. The northernmost people of all, the Lapps of Finland and their cousins, the Samoyeds of Russia, are actually the scattered remnants of the Uralians, an ancient group once spread right across the tundra of Europe and Asia. Their beliefs remained similar to those held by the tribespeople of Siberia until quite recent times. For the purpose of this book these traditions have been grouped together under the generic term, Norse.

It is a fact that the overwhelming bulk of mythology surviving from northern and eastern Europe is Scandinavian and Icelandic in origin. Most Slavic gods are not much more than names, and the little we know about their worship is usually as a consequence of its Christian termination. In Russia the conversion of Vladimir in 989 to the Orthodox faith involved the ransacking of pagan temples at Kiev. Fortunately, chroniclers of this event noted the strange worship accorded to the thunder god Perunu or Veles, the god of flocks. Without such passing testimony our scant knowledge would be almost nonexistent. Even so, there are difficulties with Vladimir's own pagan beliefs prior to his conversion to Christianity. He was of Swedish descent and the "Rus" state he ruled on the River Dnieper was a by-product of Viking exploration. It is therefore likely that the Slavic thunder god Perunu had already absorbed much of Thor's mythology. Although a native hammer-god undoubtedly existed before the Vikings arrived in the 860s, the importance of northern warriors in Novgorod and Kiev made it inevitable that the Russian god would be identified with his Germanic counterpart. The strength of the Viking presence can be judged from the Arab traveller Ibn-Fadlan's account of the ship cremation of a "Rus" leader on the Volga river in 922.

In the Balkans the Slavs not only encountered Orthodox Christianity, but were later for a time under Islamic rule also. This long isolation from such Slavonic influences did not bode well for Balkan mythology. As the myths were never written down, the influence of Christianity and Islamic rule replaced the native story-telling. Of Baltic mythology next to nothing now exists, although some idea can be formed of the pantheon. The brutal truth is that European mythology has escaped the Baltic fate only where by historical accident it was written down. In the case of Celtic

ODIN, the leading warrior god of the Vikings, at left, bears the weapons of his warcraft, an axe and spear. The stylized tree depicted beside him symbolizes Yggdrasil, the World Tree. At centre is the thunder god Thor, wielding his fiery thunderbolt, Mjollnir; while at right, Freyr bears an ear of corn to represent his fertility. (TAPESTRY, 12TH CENTURY.)

mythology we are fortunate in the care taken by Christian monks in Ireland to record the ancient sagas. The classical heritage of Greece and Rome was preserved like that of the Celts in monastic libraries, after the Germanic peoples overran the western provinces of the Roman empire. And much of Germanic mythology would have been lost in its turn without the efforts of the Icelandic scholar and statesman Snorri Sturluson.

At the turn of the thirteenth century Snorri Sturluson wrote a handbook for poets on the world of the Germanic gods, providing detailed explanations of the old myths. He was recalling the sagas of the Viking era, approximately 750–1050, when a vigorous tradition formed around the heroic deeds of Odin, Thor and Freyr. Still untouched by Christianity, the restless and adventurous Northmen – the Danes, Norwegians and Swedes – put to sea in search of plunder and land. Viking warriors were largely organized in small bands or ships' crews, only joining together in temporary alliances for military expeditions, trading voyages or piracy. They might serve under a famous leader for a while, and then break up again, although on occasion they built up armies or large fleets of warships, like the forces that attacked France in 842 or invaded England in 866. Their magnificent ships and expert seamanship gave them mastery of rivers and seas, and enabled them to travel far and wide.

The Irish lamented the Viking onslaught most. "The sea spewed forth floods of foreigners over Ireland," noted the *Annals of Ulster*, "so that no harbour, no beach, no stronghold, no fort, no castle, might be found, but it was sunk beneath waves of northmen and pirates." In 836 the Vikings had decided to set up a permanent raiding base on the site of present-day Dublin.

It is hardly surprising that aggressive Viking

SIGURD roasts the heart of the terrible dragon, Fafnir, and sucks his thumb which was splashed with the dragon's blood. On tasting the otherworldly blood, Sigurd gained the power to understand birdsong and learnt from the birds that Regin, his tutor sleeping by the fire, planned treachery. (WOOD CARVING, 12TH CENTURY.)

warriors loved hearing about the exploits of one-eyed Odin. This chief of the Germanic gods exerted a special fascination as "father of the slain". He shared those who fell on the battlefield with Freyja, the goddess of fertility. He also inspired the frightful berserkers, the shield-biting fighters who rushed unheeding and naked into the fray. When the Danish king Harald Wartooth complained about Odin's fickleness, the way he gave luck in battle and then suddenly withdrew it again,

the war god said "the grey wolf watches the halls of the gods". Gathering to Valhalla the heroic warriors slain in battle was the only policy Odin felt he could sensibly follow under the constant threat of Ragnarok, the doom of the gods. These dead warriors, the *Einherjar*, were desperately needed for the final battle on the Vigrid Plain, where nearly all would fall in an encounter between the gods and the frost giants. Odin himself was destined to be killed by the wolf Fenrir, the monstrous offspring of the fire god Loki and the frost giantess Angrboda. Whether Harald Wartooth accepted this as an adequate answer is uncertain, since Odin, who was acting as his charioteer, flung the old king down and slew him with his sword as he fell.

VALHALLA (below), the splendid, many-spired Hall of the Slain, housed Odin's phantom army of heroic warriors, gathered to fight at Ragnarok – the preordained doom of the gods. On the right, the massive World Serpent, Jormungand, was destined to overwhelm the world at Ragnarok. (ILLUSTRATION FROM THE PROSE EDDA, 1760.)

The "axe-age, sword-age", which was the age that would lead up to the catastrophe of Ragnarok, must have seemed like a description of contemporary times to the footloose Vikings. But for those who settled down as colonists, either as farmers or traders, an alternative god to worship was Thor, Odin's son. Although "allergic" to frost giants, Thor is represented in the sagas as an honest and straightforward person. He was very popular with Icelandic colonists, who had fled southern Norway to avoid the Odin-like activities of leaders like Erik Bloodaxe. Thousands of them revealed their allegiance in the choice of family name: Thorsten or Thorolf were most common. Thor was indeed a reassuring supernatural presence in both divine and human crises, be they encroachments by frost giants on gods, or local tyrants on farmers, or even overzealous Christian missionaries on pagan temples. Ever handy was his thunderhammer Mjollnir, a magic instrument with powers of destruction, fertility and resurrection. It was hardly surprising then that Thor became a greater god than Odin at the close of the Viking era, just a century or so before Scandinavia was converted to Christianity.

LOKI (below), the fiery trickster god, was to begin with a mischievous and playful prankster, but he became so dark and twisted that his malice threatened the stability of the world and precipitated Ragnarok. Here, the troublesome god taunts the Rhine Maidens, who are grieving the loss of their Rhinegold. (ILLUSTRATION BY ARTHUR RACKHAM, C. 1900.)

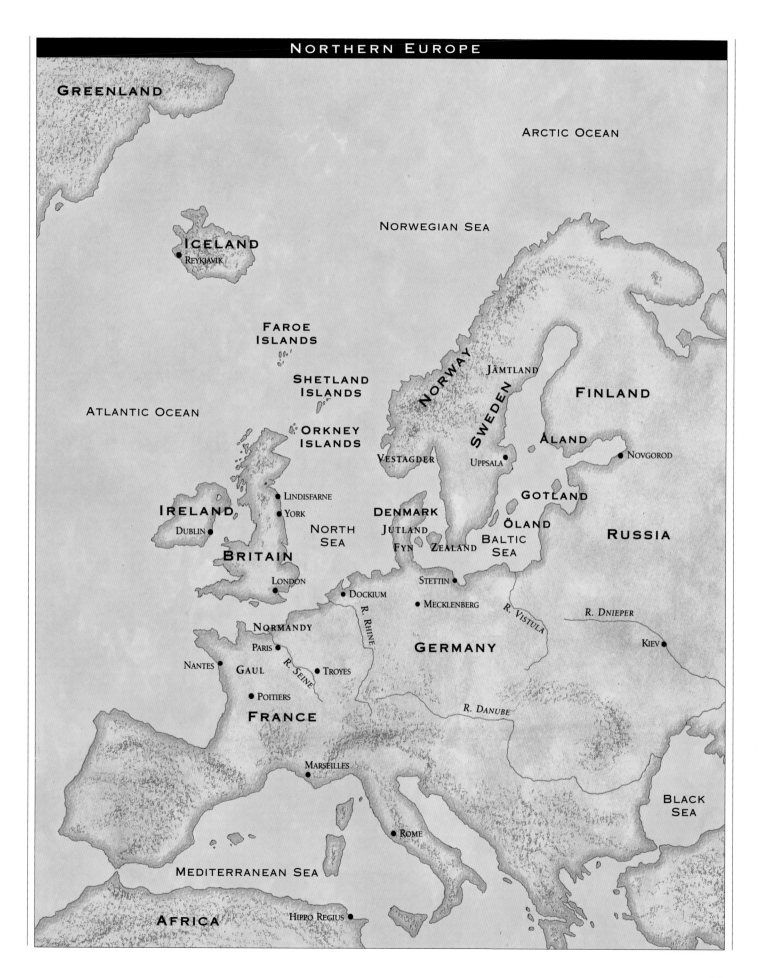

NORTHERN EUROPE

A

AEGIR, or Eagor, was a Germanic sea god, the husband of *RAN* and father of nine daughters, the waves. He seems to have belonged to an older generation of the gods than either the *AESIR* or the *VANIR*, although no details of his descent survive. Aegir was sometimes depicted as a very old man with white hair and claw-like fingers. Whenever he rose from his underwater hall, he broke the surface of the sea for a single purpose, the destruction of ships and their crews. To ensure a calm voyage, prisoners would usually be sacrificed to Aegir before a Viking raiding party set sail for home.

One myth tells how the proud sea god was outwitted by *THOR*. Aegir had been ordered by Thor to brew some ale for the gods, but he pretended that he had no cauldron large enough for the task. In fact he disliked being told what to do. But undaunted, Thor acquired a vast cauldron from the frost giant *HYMIR*. It was so big that when he hoisted it onto his shoulders, the

AEGIR (above), a tempestuous and powerful god of the sea, resided in a glistening underwater palace from where he directed the swirling waves through his nine daughters, who were known as the billow maidens. The hissing, seething Nordic sea was called "Aegir's Brewing Kettle". (ILLUSTRATION BY JAMES ALEXANDER, 1995.)

AEGIR'S sister-wife, Ran, was famous for her drowning net, which she used to snatch unsuspecting sailors from the decks of ships and drag them down to the seabed. She entertained them in her coral caves, which were lit by gleaming gold and where mead flowed as freely as in Valhalla. (ILLUSTRATION BY PETER HURD, 1882.)

handles reached his ankles. Hymir tried to stop Thor leaving with the cauldron, but the god's hammer saw off Hymir and his gigantic friends. As a result, a humiliated Aegir had to accept the cauldron and supply *ASGARD*, the home of the gods, with ale.

It was at a subsequent feast for the gods held by Aegir that *LOKI* showed how evil he had become when he insulted the assembled company and stabbed Aegir's servant Fimafeng.

THE AESIR, in Germanic mythology, were one branch of the family of the gods; the other branch were the *VANIR*. At one time there was a war between the younger Aesir and the older Vanir, which ended in a peace that left the Aesir dominant. Both branches had in fact grown weary of fighting, and were pleased to come to terms. In order to cement the peace, several of the leading Aesir went to live among the Vanir, while a number of important Vanir went to *ASGARD*, the Aesir's home.

The Aesir, under the leadership of *ODIN*, included his sons *BALDER* ("the bleeding god") and *BRAGI*, the god of eloquence; the justice god *FORSETI*, who resolved quarrels in a splendid hall supported by pillars of red gold and covered with a roof inlaid with silver; the fertility god *FREYR*, once a leading Vanir; the vigilant *HEIMDALL*, whose duty it would be to summon every living creature to *RAGNAROK*, the day of doom, with his horn; blind *HODR*, the unwitting killer of Balder; the trickster *LOKI*, god of fire and ally of the frost giants; the sea god *NJORD*, one of the gods exchanged with the Vanir; another of Odin's sons, *THOR*, whose mighty magic hammer was the only weapon the frost giants feared; the god of war *TYR*, a son of Hymir; *VILI* and *VE*, the brothers of Odin; and *VIDAR*, a son of Odin who was destined to avenge his father's death at Ragnarok.

The goddesses of the Aesir were *FREYJA*, the fertility goddess and twin sister of Freyr; *FRIGG*, Odin's wife; *SIF*, the wife of Thor; and *IDUN*, who was the keeper of the apples of youth.

Almost all the Aesir were to be killed at Ragnarok (the doom of the gods), when a terrible battle was destined to take place between the forces led by Odin, and the forces led by Loki.

ALBERICH see *ANDVARI*

ALVIS ("All Wise"), in Germanic mythology, was a dwarf who was outwitted by *ODIN*'s son *THOR*, the possessor of a magic hammer of irresistible force. In payment for the weapons Alvis had forged for them, the gods promised that he could marry Thor's daughter *THRUD*. However, Thor was displeased with the arrangement and so devised a test of knowledge to stop the dwarf from marrying his daughter. When Alvis came to *ASGARD*, Thor questioned him all night long because sunlight turned dwarfs to stone.

ALVIS, a dwarf famed for his wisdom, hoped to marry Thor's giant daughter, Thrud, but first he had to prove that his great wisdom made up for his small stature. Thor quizzed him and prolonged the test until sunrise when the first ray petrified Alvis who, like all dwarfs, turned to stone in daylight. (ILLUSTRATION BY JAMES ALEXANDER, 1995.)

THE AESIR (left) were warrior-gods worshipped by heroes and kings. Very like Norsemen, they loved, fought and died with human feelings for, though divine, they were not immortal. Odin, seen here in horned helmet, behind the Vanir twins, led the heroic Aesir. (THE NORTHERN GODS DESCENDING BY W COLLINGWOOD, CANVAS, C. 1890.)

ANDVARI'S (above) treasure trove was stolen by the gods Odin and Loki in order to pay a ransom. When they took his gold-making ring too, Andvari danced with rage and cursed the ring. At top, the three Norns examine the dark thread of destiny, while below, Hel awaits a new inmate. (ILLUSTRATION BY F VON STASSEN, 1914.)

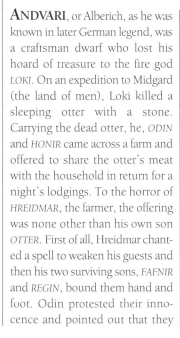

ANDVARI, or Alberich, as he was known in later German legend, was a craftsman dwarf who lost his hoard of treasure to the fire god *LOKI*. On an expedition to Midgard (the land of men), Loki killed a sleeping otter with a stone. Carrying the dead otter, he, *ODIN* and *HONIR* came across a farm and offered to share the otter's meat with the household in return for a night's lodgings. To the horror of *HREIDMAR*, the farmer, the offering was none other than his own son *OTTER*. First of all, Hreidmar chanted a spell to weaken his guests and then his two surviving sons, *FAFNIR* and *REGIN*, bound them hand and foot. Odin protested their innocence and pointed out that they

would not have come straight to the farm had they known the otter was the farmer's son. So, eventually, Hreidmar settled on a death-price: enough gold to cover Otter's skin, inside and out. Because the flayed skin was endowed with magic powers, it was capable of being stretched to a great size and so no ordinary amount of gold could be accepted in compensation.

Loki was allowed by Hreidmar to seek this great treasure, while Odin and Honir (in some versions just Honir) remained at the farm as hostages. The fire god was not permitted to wear his sky-shoes, however, and these were also kept as security against Loki's return. Having borrowed the drowning-net

of Ran, wife of the sea god *AEGIR*, Loki descended through a maze of dripping tunnels to an underground lake, where he caught a large pike. This fish, like the otter before, turned out to be more than it first seemed. For it was in fact the dwarf Andvari, who was the richest of those who dwelt underground. Only because of Loki's terrible threats, Andvari surrendered all his immense hoard of gold, including his magic gold-making ring. But in his anger the dwarf laid a terrible curse on the ring which would cause the doom of whoever wore it. When Loki returned to the farm with the gold and Odin and Honir were released, he told Hreidmar of Andvari's curse and in this way

passed it on to the farmer. Indeed, Hreidmar was soon after killed by his son Fafnir, who then ran away with the cursed treasure.

The hero *SIGURD* was later persuaded by his foster-father Regin to pursue Fafnir, who had by this time become a dragon. The hero duly searched for the creature and eventually found it in its lair and slew it. However, when Sigurd realized that for the sake of the treasure Regin intended to kill him in turn, he made sure that he slew his foster-father first. Thus it was that Andvari's curse continued to cling to the stolen gold and brought about the death of all those who attempted to possess it. (See also *RINGS OF POWER*)

A

the sun and the moon, as his price for the eighteen-month task. At *LOKI*'s suggestion, *ODIN* set the seemingly impossible limit of six months for the construction of Asgard's walls. As a concession the stonemason was allowed to use his horse, the magic Svadilfari, to help him in the work. To the horror of the gods he had finished all the walls, except a gateway, three days before the time was up. So Loki transformed himself into a mare and beguiled the stonemason's stallion, thus preventing the completion of the job. The stonemason then revealed himself as a frost giant and *THOR* broke his skull with his hammer. It is ironic that the defences of Asgard should have been built by the labour of a frost giant, given the bitter enmity between the gods and the giants. Indeed, at *RAGNAROK* these two enemies were destined to meet in a battle of mutual destruction.

The idea of city walls that were built by giants is a widespread myth in Europe. The walls of Tiryns in southern Greece, for example, were believed to have been constructed by the Cyclopes, who were giant, one-eyed beings. There is also a story of a dispute over payment for the strengthening of Troy's walls by the gods Apollo and Poseidon and King Laomedon, which is not dissimilar to the above story concerning Asgard's walls. (See also *RAGNAROK*)

ANGRBODA, or Angerboda ("Distress-bringer"), in Germanic mythology, was a frost giantess. She was the mistress of *LOKI* and the mother of three monstrous offspring: the wolf *FENRIR*, the serpent *JORMUNGAND*, and a daughter named *HEL*. When the gods heard about this brood, they agreed that such creatures must be dealt with quickly. A group of gods broke into Angrboda's hall at night, bound and gagged her, and took her and Loki's children to *ASGARD*.

ODIN first banished Hel to the "world beneath the worlds" and there he put her in charge of all the inglorious dead. He then hurled Jormungand into the ocean, where the huge snake smashed through the ice and sank down into the depths. Odin was less certain what to do with Fenrir, so at first he decided that the gods should keep an eye on him at Asgard. However, when the *NORNS*, the goddesses of destiny, warned that the wolf would bring about Odin's death action was finally taken to bind Fenrir securely with a magic chain and keep him in captivity.

Although Angrboda's children were thus contained, Odin knew that the wolf Fenrir would break free at *RAGNAROK*, the day of doom, and destroy him. The sea serpent Jormungand also awaited the final conflict, like his sister Hel "surrounded by corpses and swirling death-mist" in the netherworld. A tenth-century Danish complaint about Odin's withdrawal of luck from brave warriors is answered in terms of Angrboda's brood. Odin is supposed to have said that "the

grey wolf watches the halls of the gods". With this threat in mind, he had no choice but to gather to his side the greatest champions.

ASGARD, in Germanic mythology, was the divine stronghold of the *AESIR*, who were the younger and stronger branch of the family of gods. The other branch, the *VANIR*, lived in Vanaheim. Asgard's mighty walls were built by a stonemason, Hrimthurs, who named the hand of the fertility goddess *FREYJA*, plus

AUDHUMLA was the primeval cow in Germanic mythology. This creature was the first animal to emerge from *GINNUNGAGAP* ("the yawning emptiness") at the start of creation. From Audhumla's teats "flowed four rivers of milk", nourishment enough for *YMIR*, the first frost giant and the first live thing of all. From Ymir's children descended the frost giants, the implacable enemies of the gods. The cow herself seems to have survived on the goodness that she obtained from an icy salt lick. As she licked, first some hair appeared, then a head, and finally the whole body of a man, *BURI*. In time Buri had a son named *BOR*, who married Bestla, the daughter of a frost giant. Their sons were the first gods, *ODIN*, *VILI* and *VE*. These three battled against the frost giants and finally slew Ymir. As the giant fell the blood from his wounds flooded the land and drowned all his frost children, except for *BERGELMIR* and his wife who managed to escape.

BABA YAGA, sometimes Jezi Baba, is the hideous man-eating female demon of Slavonic tradition. According to some versions of her myth, her mouth is said to stretch from earth to the gates of hell. She lived in a strange house which had legs like a chicken's at each corner, and stood inside a fence made of human bones. When she wished to travel, it was believed that she flew in an iron kettle.

ASGARD, (above) the magnificent stronghold of the Aesir gods, shimmered on a plane above Midgard. Within, there were countless shining, glittering halls for each of the gods. Asgard was linked to Midgard by an ethereal pathway for the gods, a wondrous rainbow bridge called Bifrost. (ILLUSTRATION BY ALAN LEE, 1984.)

AUDHUMLA (below), the original cow, emerged from the primal ice at the dawn of time, and nourished the first frost giant, Ymir. She survived by licking ice from which she freed the first man, Buri. Here, while Ymir suckles her milk, Audhumla licks Buri free of the ice. (AUDHUMLA BY N A ABILGAARD, CANVAS, C. 1790.)

BABA YAGA (bottom right) was a Slavonic witch of monstrous size who preyed on travellers, devouring their flesh with a mouth that stretched from earth to hell. She was seen as a hunched hag, bearded, part-woman, part-tree. Here, perched on a rolling log, she propells herself forward with a pole. (ILLUSTRATION BY I BILIBIN, 1900.)

15

BALDER, sometimes Baldr or Baldur, was the son of *ODIN* and *FRIGG* and the "bleeding god" of Germanic mythology. His wife was Nanna and their son, *FORSETI*, was the god of justice.

As a young man, Balder was tormented by nightmares, all of which indicated that he was about to die. A sense of foreboding, therefore, settled over *ASGARD*, the home of the gods, as the divine inhabitants tried to understand the meaning of Balder's dreams. They were deeply puzzled because the gentle god least deserved to suffer such torments. So Odin rode his eight-legged steed *SLEIPNIR* to the land of the dead and by means of magic learned from a seeress there that Balder was to be killed by the blind god *HODR*, his own brother, with a branch. Although depressed by this news, Odin returned to Asgard and found that his wife Frigg had a plan to save Balder. The goddess

travelled through the nine worlds and got each and every thing to swear an oath that it would do her son no harm. To Odin's relief this plan seemed to work. When the

BALDER, a loving and gentle soul, spread light and goodwill wherever he went but, inevitably, evoked the envy of the bitter god Loki, who plotted his tragic death and imprisonment in Hel. This romantic portrayal captures the sacred, Christ-like goodness of the god.
(BALDER BY B FOGELBERG, MARBLE, 1840.)

gods decided to test Balder's new invulnerability by throwing stones and spears at him with great force, he remained unharmed. All in Asgard were delighted except *LOKI*, the god of fire. He was so annoyed by Balder's escape from danger that he transformed himself into an old woman and visited Frigg's hall. In conversation with the goddess, Loki learned that she had received a promise of harmlessness from all things except the mistletoe, which was a plant too small and too feeble to bother about.

Armed with this information, Loki went off to cut some mistletoe. In his normal shape the fire

god returned to the assembly of the gods and found everyone throwing things at Balder, except blind Hodr. Pretending to help Hodr enjoy the sport, Loki gave him the branch of mistletoe and directed his throw, with the result that the branch passed right through Balder, who immediately fell down dead. At Frigg's entreaty *HERMOD*, Balder's brother, was sent to *HEL* in order to offer a ransom for Balder. He used the eight-legged Sleipnir for the journey. While Hermod was away, the bodies of Balder and Nanna, who had died of grief, were placed on a pyre in a longship which was allowed to drift burning out to sea.

BALDER's body was laid on a pyre in his longship and he was then covered in treasure and decorated with flowers and thorns, the emblems of sleep. His ship was set aflame and pushed out to sea where it shone brightly, before sinking into darkness.
(FUNERAL OF A VIKING BY F DICKSEE, CANVAS, 1893.)

In the netherworld the brave Hermod found his brother Balder seated in a high position. When he asked for his release, Hel said Balder could leave only on condition that "everything in the nine worlds, dead and alive, wept for him". Messengers were sent out and soon even the stones were weeping. But THOKK, an old frost giantess, refused, saying, "Let Hel hold what she has." So upset were the gods at this refusal to mourn that it took some time for them to realize that Thokk was none other than Loki in disguise. Nevertheless, Balder remained with Hel.

Balder's good looks and early death recall the myths of the Egyptian Osiris and the Sumerian Tammuz, as well as that of Adonis, who was the dying-and-rising god the ancient Greeks adopted from the Phoenicians. For the Germanic peoples believed that the return of the wounded, dying Balder would occur in a new world, a green land risen from the sea, after RAGNAROK, the doom of the gods. Like the undead Celtic King Arthur, Balder was expected to return and rule over a world cleansed by catastrophe. It would seem that some of the initial appeal of Christianity in northern Europe was connected with the triumphant return of the risen Christ on Judgement Day. (See also RAGNAROK)

BALDR see BALDER

BALDUR see BALDER

BEOWULF was the Germanic hero who slew two water monsters. He was said to be the nephew of the king of Geats, whom some interpret as the Jutes. His story is set in Denmark. One night a dreadful creature known as *GRENDEL* came to the hall of King Hrothgar and ate one of the warriors sleeping there. Although invulnerable to weapons, Grendel was seized by Beowulf and held in a powerful grip, from which it could only

BEOWULF, seen here with raised drinking horn, gazes up at the gory trophy hanging from the splendid vault of Denmark's Victory Hall. The giant hairy hand belonged to the fearsome sea monster, Grendel, who had continually terrorized and devoured the Danes, until Beowulf tore the creature's arm right out of its socket. (ILLUSTRATION BY ALAN LEE, 1984.)

BEOWULF wrestles with a monstrous merwoman in the crystal cavern of her underwater den. Grieving for the death of her son, Grendel, slain by Beowulf, the merwoman fought with frenzy, but Beowulf battled calmly and took her by surprise. (ILLUSTRATION BY JAMES ALEXANDER, 1995.)

break away by losing an arm. Mortally wounded, the water monster fled to its home, deep in a nearby lake, and bled to death.

Delighted by this feat of courage and strength, King Hrothgar loaded Beowulf with gifts, since his kingdom had been rid of a menace. But neither the king nor the warrior reckoned on Grendel's mother, an even more dreadful creature. She returned to the attack and ate another sleeping warrior. In pursuit, Beowulf followed her into a lake and dived down to her cavernlike lair. A desperate struggle then took place and Beowulf lost his

trusty sword. Like Arthur, he was fortunate to find another magic weapon in the water and he used this to finish off Grendel's mother.

Having once again saved King Hrothgar's kingdom from danger, Beowulf returned home to southern Sweden, where his father ruled. Towards the end of his popular reign a dragon attacked his land. Going out with twelve followers to slay the fiery beast, Beowulf soon found himself almost on his own, for all his companions but one ran away in terror. Although he managed to kill the dragon, it was at the cost of his own life.

In contrast to the Celtic myths that describe combat with watergiants, the Germanic stories tell of heroes who face actual monsters rather than magical opponents. This is quite unlike the great Ulster hero and champion Cuchulainn's beheading contest with Uath, or Sir Gawain's with the Green Knight, for in these traditions their monstrous opponents were able to restore themselves to life after they had been decapitated.

BEOWULF, even in his old age, tackled fire-breathing dragons. Yet neither his might nor his fabled armour, crafted by Wayland, could withstand the dragon's crushing teeth. Beowulf was mortally wounded in the combat, but he did not die before seeing the dragon's treasure released for his people. (ILLUSTRATION BY JAMES ALEXANDER, 1995.)

BERGELMIR, according to Germanic mythology, was the son of Thrudgelmir and the grandson of *YMIR*. When *ODIN*, *VILI* and *VE* killed Ymir and threw his body into the middle of *GINNUNGAGAP*, all the frost giants drowned in the giant's blood except Bergelmir and his wife. By using a hollowed tree trunk as a boat, they escaped to

BIFROST (above) was a gigantic rainbow causeway, reaching from the shining citadel of Asgard to the earthly realm of Midgard. Composed of fire, water and air, it shimmered with rainbow-coloured light in hues of red, blue and green. Over the ethereal arch, the gods moved to and fro. (ILLUSTRATION BY ALAN LEE, 1984.)

continue the race of giants, who never lost their hatred for the gods. At *RAGNAROK* the frost giants and the dead of *HEL* were destined to settle the final account for Ymir's dismemberment.

BIFROST, in Germanic mythology, was the flaming three-strand rainbow bridge between *ASGARD* and Midgard (heaven and earth respectively). It was said to have been built by the gods out of red fire, green water and blue air, and was guarded by the watchman god *HEIMDALL*. Every day the gods rode across the bridge to hold meetings at the well of *URD*.

BILLING, in Germanic mythology, was the father of *RIND*. According to some traditions, he was king of the Ruthenians, or Russians. So strong-willed was Rind that *ODIN* could not woo her, even though Billing approved of the god's suit. On the contrary, she treated the chief of the Germanic gods with undisguised contempt. Eventually, however, she gave way to his advances and she bore a son, *VALI*, who killed *HODR* with his bow and arrow.

BERGELMIR (below) and his wife were the only frost giants to escape drowning in the torrent of Ymir's blood that flowed from his mortal wounds. They journeyed in a hollowed-out tree trunk to the edge of the world where they founded the realm of Jotunheim and bred a new race of giants. (ILLUSTRATION BY NICK BEALE, 1995.)

BILLING (above) gazes in wonder at the glittering trinkets fashioned by the dwarf goldsmith Rosterus. Unknown to King Billing, the dwarf is Odin in disguise, who was intent on wooing the king's daughter, Rind. She was destined to bear Odin a son, Vali, who would avenge Balder's death. (ILLUSTRATION BY NICK BEALE, 1995.)

BOR was the son of *BURI*, husband of the giant Bestla and father of *ODIN*, *VILI* and *VE*. An ancient god, Bor lived in the time before the world had been made, when there was no earth, sky or sea, only mist, ice, fire and the gaping pit of *GINNUNGAGAP*. Bor's father-in-law, the giant Bolthur, also had a son who imparted his wisdom to his nephew Odin.

BRAGI was the son of *ODIN* and Gunnlod, a female giant, and was the Germanic god of poetry and eloquence. He was married to *IDUN*, the goddess who kept the magic apples of youth. When *LOKI* returned to *ASGARD*, after being instrumental in causing *BALDER*'s death, Bragi, who was never at a loss for words, told him that he was

BRAGI (above) was born in a glittering stalactite cave, where his mother, Gunnlod, guarded the Mead of Poetry, until seduced by Odin. The dwarfs gave the fair child a magical harp and set him afloat on one of their fine-crafted vessels from which he sang his poignant Song of Life which rose to the heavens. (ILLUSTRATION BY PETER HURD, 1882.)

unwelcome company at their feast. Enraged, Loki called Bragi "the bragger", whereupon Bragi threatened to twist off Loki's head as the only sure method of stopping his lies. Although Odin tried to calm the gathering, the effect of Bragi's words on Loki was to make him

THE BRISINGAMEN (below) was an exquisite necklace crafted by dwarfs so finely that it shone like liquid flame. The goddess Freyja, beside herself with longing, paid dearly for possessing the treasure. An emblem of the stars, it so enhanced her beauty that she wore it continually, night and day. (ILLUSTRATION BY J PENROSE, C. 1890.)

even more threatening. He finally prophesied the destruction of the gods and then fled from Asgard.

Possibly Bragi was a late addition to the Germanic pantheon. It is not unlikely that Bragi was added through the divine elevation of a poet, since in Germanic courts poets were venerated second only to kings. Bragi was portrayed as an old, bearded man carrying a harp, and when oaths were sworn they were solemnized by speaking over a vessel called the Cup of Bragi.

BRISINGAMEN see RINGS OF POWER

THE BRISINGS, also known as the Bristlings, were the mysterious owners of a golden necklace, called the Brisingamen, that the fertility goddess *FREYJA* craved. To *ODIN*'s disgust she slept on four successive nights with the dwarfs Alfrigg, Dvalin, Berling and Grer in order to acquire it. When she returned to *ASGARD*, Odin accused her of debasing her divinity by paying such a price. As a penance he made her stir up war in Midgard, the world of men. Freyja and Odin shared those slain on the battlefield.

No agreement exists about the meaning of this strange myth, not least because the identity of the Brisings is unknown. It has been suggested that necklaces were the special adornment of mother goddesses, but this hardly does more than explain Freyja's attraction to this particular one. What seems more likely is that the sexual price Freyja paid for it represents the other side of love, namely, blind passion and lust. Nothing could stop her, not even Odin's great disapproval, when she desired something badly enough. The Brisingamen came to be identified so closely with Freyja that when *THOR* wished to disguise himself as the goddess to retrieve his hammer from *THRYM*, she lent it to him to make his costume convincing. (See also *TREASURES AND TALISMANS*)

THE BRISTLINGS see BRISINGS

BRUNHILD see BRYNHILD

BRYNHILD was a *VALKYRIE* who defied *ODIN* and so was banished to earth and imprisoned within a ring of fire. When *SIGURD* braved the fire and broke her charmed sleep, they fell in love. He gave her his ring, Andvarinaut, unaware of its curse. On his travels he was bewitched by Grimhild into betraying Brynhild, first by marrying Gudrun and then by helping Gunner win Brynhild. On discovering Sigurd's betrayal, Brynhild planned his death, but then killed herself in despair. (See also *THE VALKYRIES*; *TRAGIC LOVERS*)

BURI, in Germanic mythology, was the ancestor of the gods. He was released from the ice by *AUDHUMLA*, the primeval cow. One day Buri's hair appeared where she licked; on the second day, his head was free of ice; and, on the third, his entire body. He had a son, *BOR*, who married a frost giantess, and their sons were *ODIN*, *VILI* and *VE*.

BRYNHILD, one of the leading Valkyries, was punished by Odin for meddling with his will in warfare. The god put her to sleep and imprisoned her in a ring of fire, where she would remain until a peerless hero freed her. Only Sigurd braved the scorching fire, waking her from her enchanted sleep. (ILLUSTRATION BY ARTHUR RACKHAM, C.1900.)

NATURE SPIRITS

THE DRAMATIC LANDSCAPE of Scandinavia, with its electric skies, icy wastes and seething springs, was easily peopled with nature spirits. Such spirits roamed the mountains and snow slopes as fearsome frost, storm and fire giants, personifying the mysterious and menacing forces of nature. So great were the terrors of crushing ice and searing fire that the giants loomed large in the Norse myths as evil and ominous forces. Yet other less dramatic but no less important spirits were the invisible *landvaettir*, or land spirits, who imbued the land and guarded its welfare. Helpful and timid, the *landvaettir* easily took fright, shying away from Viking dragon ships. In the underground caverns, dark dwarfs unearthed glittering gems and metals, while light elves inspired the forests and lakes. In Slavonic myth, a host of vital forces filled the world and imbued the forests, fields and rivers with whirling spirits of nature.

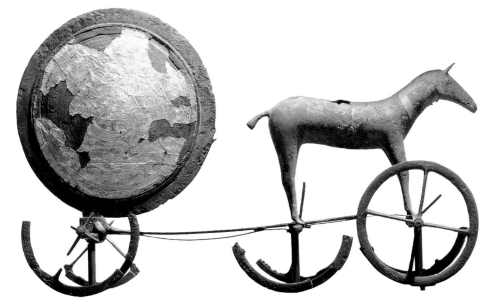

THE FROST GIANTS (below) personified the icy terrors of the Nordic landscape. Mighty, menacing and numbing, the ice masses of the North were a constant threat to the Norsemen, much like the frost giants, whose undying enmity would overwhelm the gods at Ragnarok. In the interim, the frost giants sent freezing blasts to nip the buds of spring, or shook avalanches from their icy shoulders and brows. (RONDANE AT NIGHT BY H SOHLBERG, CANVAS, C. 1890.)

THE SUN (above), in one myth, was fashioned by the gods from a bright spark of fire. Its glowing orb was placed in a chariot, drawn by two white steeds and driven by the sun-maid, Sol. Fearing that the sun's heat might be harmful, the gods placed a shield, Svalin, or Cooler, in front of the golden car. In another myth, the gods gave a giant, Day, a chariot and horses to drive round the earth once every 24 hours. Day's horse, Shining Mane, lit up the earth and sky with the radiance of his shining hair. (SUN DISC, GILDED BRONZE, C. 1000 BC.)

RAN (left), a stormy spirit of the sea, reflected the shifting moods of the ocean, sometimes helpful, sometimes harmful. She gathered sailors in her drowning net and dragged them down to the depths of the sea. There, with her husband, Aegir, she entertained her victims in her gleaming coral caves, which were lit by the shining gold of the sea. Ran loved gold, named the Flame of the Sea, after the fluorescent quality of Nordic waves. Sailors seeking Ran's favour wisely pocketed some gold for the trip. (ILLUSTRATION BY ARTHUR RACKHAM, C. 1900.)

DARK DWARFS (below) were formed from maggots in the rotting flesh of the slain giant, Ymir. The gods thought them too ugly to be seen, however, and condemned them to a life underground. Like giants, they turned to stone in daylight, thus explaining the many smaller stones and rocks scattered across the Nordic landscape. The twin peaks of Trold Tindterne, for example, are two bands of warring dwarfs who forgot to retreat before sunrise. As dwarfs had a habit of whispering behind rocks, the mountain echoes were known as "dwarfs' talk". (ILLUSTRATION BY ALAN LEE, 1984.)

THE RHINE MAIDENS (above) were ethereal sprites who dwelt in lakes and rivers during the winter, emerging from the water to flit through the forests in summer. The river's colours reflected the nymphs' moods, turning black with grief when the Rhine Maidens lost their gold. Here, the Rhine Maidens berate their loss to the gods crossing the rainbow bridge above. (ILLUSTRATION BY ARTHUR RACKHAM, C.1900.)

ROCK AND STORM GIANTS personified the vast craggy mountains and storm clouds. Rocky chasms and outcrops were created by giants treading too heavily at the dawn of time. Best suited to mist and fog, the mountain giants, like dwarfs, were petrified by the light of day, which explains some fantastic rock formations, such as the Riesengebirge (right), formed by foolish giants who were caught outside at sunrise. Similarly, in Iceland the highest peaks are named Jokul which derives from Jotun or Giant.
(ILLUSTRATION BY NICK BEALE, 1995.)

E

DAZHBOG was the Slavic sun god, known as Dabog to the Serbs and Dazbog to the Poles. Son of Svarog, the god of the sky, and brother of *SVARAZIC*, god of fire, he was born again every morning and rode through the sky on his diamond chariot until he became an old man in the evening. In some versions he is married to *MYESYATS*, the moon, and quarrels between them are said to cause earthquakes.

DRAUPNIR see *RINGS OF POWER*

DIETRICH see *RINGS OF POWER*

EAGOR see *AEGIR*

THE EINHERJAR were the "heroic dead" of Germanic mythology. They were gathered from the battlefields by the *VALKYRIES*. In *VALHALLA*, the Einherjar formed *ODIN*'s private army, which he raised to fight at *RAGNAROK*, the doom of the gods. This was the final battle between the gods and the frost giants on the *VIGRID* Plain. Until then, these dead warriors would fight every day and feast every night, and any wounds they sustained were magically healed. (See also *THE VALKYRIES*)

FAFNIR slays his father, Hreidmar, because he is bewitched by the treasure trove stolen from the dwarf Andvari. The dwarf's cursed ring can be seen glittering on Hreidmar's forefinger as he writhes in the dust. Behind the warring pair, the gods gaze on in numb dismay. (ILLUSTRATION BY F VON STASSEN, 1914.)

FAFNIR, son of the magician *HREIDMAR*, was corrupted by the cursed ring Andvarinaut. Lusting after the fabulous ring-hoard, he slew his father, helped by his brother *REGIN*. Greed made him monstrous in nature and form, as he turned into a dragon to guard his hoard. The legend of his treasure drew many aspiring heroes to his lair in search of fame and fortune. Most met their deaths on the blasted heath outside his lair, but the youthful *SIGURD*, armed with his father's sword and guided by Regin, outwitted the dragon and won his ill-fated treasure.

FARBAUTI ("Cruel striker") was a giant and father of the fire god *LOKI*. According to one tradition, his wife was another giant, Laufey ("Tree island") who gave birth to Loki when hit by a lightning bolt unleashed by Farbauti. Little else is known of Loki's parents.

FENRIR, or Fenris, according to Germanic mythology, was the son of the mischief-making god *LOKI* and the frost giantess *ANGRBODA*. He was the devouring wolf, the beast of *RAGNAROK*, the doom of the gods. His was "an axe-age, a sword-age, a wind-age, a wolf-age, before the wrecking of the world". *ODIN*, the chief of the gods, was destined to become his victim.

Kidnapped by the gods and brought to *ASGARD* where they could keep an eye on him, Fenrir was so savage that only the war god *TYR* dared to feed him. At first Odin was uncertain about the wolf, but when the *NORNS*, the goddesses of destiny, warned him about his own fate, he decided that Fenrir should be restrained. No chain, however, was strong enough to hold the animal. Finally, the dwarfs made a magic fetter called Gleipnir from strange materials such as the roots of a mountain and bird's spittle. Although it seemed to be a silken ribbon, Fenrir would not have it round his neck unless one of the gods put his hand between his jaws as a pledge that it was as harmless as it seemed. Tyr was the only one prepared to risk his hand, and the other gods laughed when the wolf bit it off on finding that the chain could not be broken. Fenrir was then secured to a rock and his

THE EINHERJAR, or "heroic dead", were gathered up from the battlefield by the Valkyries who galloped over the fray, choosing the bravest heroes for Odin's ghostly army. A chosen hero saw a soaring Valkyrie just before the fatal blow. (THE RIDE OF THE VALKYRIES BY W T MAUD, CANVAS, C. 1890.)

mouth was kept open by a sword so he could not bite.

When freed from captivity at Ragnarok, Fenrir was a fearsome spectacle. His vast mouth gaped so wide that the lower jaw touched the ground and the upper one reached the sky, and Odin was swallowed by him.

FENRIS see *FENRIR*

FJALAR and his brother Galar, in Germanic mythology, were the wicked dwarfs who killed the wise man *KVASIR* in order to gain his magic powers. They mixed his blood with honey in a cauldron and made a mead that bestowed wisdom. But Fjalar and Galar lost the wonderful drink to Suttung, a frost giant whose parents they had also killed. Unlike the dwarfs, Suttung was boastful about his

FENRIR (above), the wolf fathered by Loki, was so savage that the gods chained him to an underground rock. Only a magical cord was strong enough to bind him. Here, the brave god Tyr fetters Fenrir at the cost of his own hand, which he placed in the wolf's mouth as a sign of trust. (DIE, 8TH CENTURY.)

FJALAR (below) and his brother Galar slew the wise Kvasir and drained his blood to extract his wisdom. Two glistening bowls and the Kettle of Inspiration contained the magical fluid, which the brothers mixed with honey to produce the golden Mead of Poetry. (ILLUSTRATION BY JAMES ALEXANDER, 1995.)

acquisition and it was not long before the gods heard about the mead. ODIN himself decided that he would go to JOTUNHEIM, the land of the frost giants, and lay hold of the magic drink. Disguised as evil Bolverk, he journeyed to Jotunheim and persuaded the frost giant Baugi to tunnel through a mountain to where Suttung kept the mead under the care of his daughter Gunnlod. Once the hole was drilled, Odin changed his shape from Bolverk's to a snake, and slithered downwards to the hidden treasure as quickly as he could. Reaching the secret cave, he changed himself into a handsome one-eyed giant and for three days and nights he was Gunnlod's lover. The passionate giantess let Odin drink up every drop of the mead, before he turned himself into an eagle and flew back to ASGARD, the home of the gods. There he spat the mead into jars left empty for his return. Suttung gave chase as another eagle, but just failed to catch Odin.

In the account of Kvasir's death, it is clear that this is a myth about

FORSETI, the fair god of justice, was a Solomon-like force for peace. He sat in judgement in his golden hall, Glitnir, and settled the disputes of gods and men, allaying strife and resolving feuds. He never failed to reconcile even the bitterest foes. (ILLUSTRATION BY NICK BEALE, 1995.)

fermentation. To put the seal on their peace agreement the two branches of the gods, the AESIR and the VANIR, had spat into a jar, and it was from the spittle that Kvasir had been formed. Spittle, like yeast, causes fermentation, and so when Fjalar and Galar mixed Kvasir's blood with honey in a cauldron they created a magical mead. The connection between inspiration, poetry and wisdom and some form of potent drink occurs in several mythological traditions.

FORSETI was the Germanic god of justice, and was known to the Frisians as Forsite. He was the son of BALDER and Nanna. Both of his parents were killed, his father stabbed by a piece of mistletoe, thrown unwittingly by the blind god HODR, and his mother with a broken heart shortly after this tragic event. Although Forseti plays only a relatively small role in Germanic mythology, we are told in detail that his hall of Glitnir "had pillars of red gold and a roof inlaid with silver." There he sat in judgement and resolved strife.

FREA see FREYJA

FREY see FREYR

FREYA see FREYJA

F

FREYJA, the voluptuous, blue-eyed
goddess of love, rode in a chariot drawn
by cats, which were symbols of her warm
affections. Accompanied by a flock of
airborne love spirits, she toured heaven and
earth in search of her roving husband,
Odur, shedding tears of gold all the while.
(FREYJA BY N J O BLOMMER, CANVAS, 1852.)

FREYJA ("Lady"), sometimes
known as Freya or Frea, was the
daughter of the sea god NJORD in
Germanic mythology and sister of
FREYR. She was an important fertility goddess and a member of the
VANIR, one of the two branches
into which the Germanic gods were
divided. After a war the Vanir seem
to have been supplanted by the
younger AESIR, who were led by
ODIN. When peace was agreed
between the two sides, Njord went
with Freyr and Freyja to ASGARD,
where they lived with the Aesir as a
token of friendship.

Freyja's greatest treasure was
the BRISINGS' necklace, which she
obtained by sleeping with its four
dwarf makers. Her beauty won her
many admirers, including OTTAR,
whom she changed into a boar.
She was said to be a sorceress who
could fly in a falcon's skin. Some
traditions state that, on her arrival
in Asgard, she taught the gods the
spells and charms of the Vanir.

Both Odin and Freyja took an
interest in the heroic dead, dividing
the slain between them at the end
of every battle. Odin's share went
to live in VALHALLA, while Freyja's
lived in her hall, Sessrumnir. It is
possible that Freyja's lost husband
Odur, or Od, of whom nothing is
known but his name, was Odin.
For she was the goddess of lust as
well as love, a suitable partner for
Odin who was the father of battles
and the lover of destruction. (See
also SORCERY AND SPELLS)

FREYR ("Lord"), sometimes Frey,
was the twin brother of the
Germanic fertility goddess FREYJA.
Their father was NJORD, the god
associated with the wind and the
sea. Freyr, with ODIN and THOR,
was one of the principal gods. He
was mainly concerned with fertility,
having control of sunlight, rain,
fruitfulness and peace. His title of
Skirr means "shining", and the
name of the frost giantess he married, GERDA, derives from "field".
As late as 1200, Freyr's statue in
his temple at Uppsala, Sweden was
noted for the size of its penis.
Possibly for this reason the Romans
had always identified him with
Priapus, the virile son of Dionysus
and Aphrodite. Although a member of the VANIR by descent, Freyr
moved to ASGARD to live with the
AESIR, the younger branch of the
gods under the leadership of Odin,
along with his father Njord and his

FREYJA (below) flew over the earth,
sprinkling morning dew and summer
sunlight behind her. She shook spring
flowers from her golden hair and wept tears
which turned to gold, or to amber at sea.
She was so beautiful that she was wooed
and pursued by all living creatures.
(ILLUSTRATION BY F VON STASSEN, 1914.)

FREYR (right), a gentle god of summer sun and showers, was lord of the fairy realm of Alfheim, home of the Light Elves. Here, he is sailing his ship, Skidbladnir, personifying the clouds. His flashing sword, symbolizing a sunbeam, fought of its own accord. (ILLUSTRATION BY JAMES ALEXANDER, 1995.)

sister Freyja, as a gesture of goodwill that had been agreed at the end of the war between the Vanir and the Aesir.

Freyr's myth is about his wooing of Gerda, the daughter of the frost giant Gymir. When Freyr first saw Gerda he immediately fell in love with her, and because he did not know how to gain her affection he became ill. Njord became so worried about him that he asked his faithful servant Skirnir to find out what was amiss. Having learned of this love, Skirnir went to *JOTUNHEIM*, the land of the giants, taking two of Freyr's greatest treasures, his magic horse and his magic sword. The servant was instructed to bring Gerda back to Asgard, whether her father liked it or not. On reaching Gymir's hall, Skirnir tried to persuade Gerda to

FRIGG (below), a deity of the atmosphere, spun long pearly webs of cloud from her jewelled distaff which shone in the night sky as the constellation of Frigg's Spinning Wheel. Her heron plumes symbolize her discretion, while her keys signify her divine housewifery. (ILLUSTRATION BY NICK BEALE, 1995.)

declare her love for Freyr in return for "eleven of the apples of youth". She refused both this gift and Skirnir's second offer of one of Odin's arm-rings. Gerda's resolve was only strengthened further when Skirnir then threatened to decapitate her with Freyr's sword. Finally, Skirnir said that he would impose on her an unbreakable spell that would make her a permanent outcast and it was this that persuaded Gerda to pledge herself to

the fertility god with an agreement to meet Freyr in a forest in nine days' time. In this way the passion of Freyr was fulfilled, though it cost him his horse and sword which he gave to Skirnir. At *RAGNAROK*, the doom of the gods, he sorely missed his mighty magic weapon, since it could fight giants on its own. (See also *TREASURES AND TALISMANS; TRAGIC LOVERS*)

FRICKA see *FRIGG*

FRIGG, also known as Frigga, Frija and Fricka, in Germanic mythology, was the daughter of Fjorgyn, goddess of the earth and atmosphere, wife of *ODIN*, the chief of the gods, and mother of *BALDER*. She has given her name to Friday. Frigg was a fertility goddess who "will tell no fortunes, yet well she knows the fates". When Balder dreamed of impending danger, Frigg extracted a promise from each and every thing, except the mistletoe, that no harm should happen to him. Apparently, the mistletoe appeared such a harmless

plant that she did not bother about it. This proved to be a mistake because the fire god *LOKI* got the blind god *HODR* to throw a branch of mistletoe at Balder which killed him. Frigg's subsequent effort to have her son released from the land of the dead also failed, because Loki refused to mourn on behalf of Balder. Thus it would seem that Frigg was a fertility goddess not unlike the Sumerian deity Inanna, though she lacked that goddess's ability to enter the netherworld.

Frigg has much in common with *FREYJA*. Although her role as consort of Odin shows her to be a devoted wife and mother, she too possesses a falcon skin and has a great passion for gold. It is quite possible that the two goddesses had their origins in a single earth-mother deity.

FRIGGA see *FRIGG*

FRIJA see *FRIGG*

FRITHIOF see *TRAGIC LOVERS*

GEFFINN see *GEFION*

FRIGG enjoyed the privilege of sitting beside her husband, Odin, on his fabulous throne, Hlidskialf, from where the divine pair could view the nine worlds, witnessing events present and future. A paragon of silence, she never revealed her foreknowledge. (ILLUSTRATION BY H THEAKER, C. 1920.)

GEFION, also known as Gefinn and Gefjon, was a Germanic goddess of fertility akin to FREYJA, the sister of the fertility god FREYR, and FRIGG, the wife of ODIN. Appropriately for a goddess of agriculture, Gefion's name is connected with "giving". She was usually imagined as a virgin and as the protector of virgins after their deaths. However, LOKI accused Gefion of selling herself, like Freyja, for a necklace.

Her myth concerns ploughing and doubtless recalls the ancient ritual of ploughing a token strip of land each spring. Gefion, disguised as an old beggar, managed to trick King Gylfi of Sweden out of a great tract of land. In return for her hospitality, the king offered Gefion as much of his kingdom as she could plough with four oxen during one day and one night. With the aid of her four giant sons, transformed into oxen, she cut from the mainland the whole island of Zealand, part of present-day Denmark.

GEIRROD was a frost giant, the father of two daughters, GJALP and Greip, and was one of THOR's most formidable enemies. It happened that LOKI, a constant companion of Thor, had taken the form of a hawk and was captured by Geirrod. The only way Loki could avoid death was to promise to bring Thor to Geirrod's hall without his magic belt and magic hammer which protected the god against frost giants.

Because Thor trusted Loki he went with him to Geirrod's hall. Fortunately, they rested on the way at the home of a friendly giantess named GRID, and she warned Thor about the plan while Loki was asleep. She also lent the god her own magic belt of strength, magic iron gloves and magic staff. Thus equipped, Thor arrived at their destination, with Loki hanging as usual on his belt. Geirrod was not at home, but the giant's servants received the visitors. It was not long, though, before Geirrod's two

GEIRROD's (left) immense body, slain by Thor, lay in the City of the Not-Dead, shrouded in cobwebs. Beyond the sleeping giant sparkled the Chamber of Treasures full of jewels and weapons. Here came the Danish hero, Thorkill, years later, on a raid for his king. (ILLUSTRATION BY NICK BEALE, 1995.)

GEFION (above), disguised as a beggar, ploughed a vast field in Sweden with four giant oxen, her supernatural sons. They dragged the tilled field to the coast and floated it across the sea to Denmark, where it formed the island of Zealand. (ILLUSTRATION BY JAMES ALEXANDER, 1995.)

daughters tried to kill the slumbering Thor by lifting up his chair and dashing out his brains on the ceiling. But with the aid of Grid's staff, Thor succeeded in driving the chair downwards and crushed the frost giantesses instead. However, Geirrod himself then appeared in the hall and using a pair of tongs he picked up a red-hot iron ball and threw it at Thor, who caught it in Grid's iron gloves. Angered beyond measure by this extremely discourteous action, Thor threw the still hot and smoking ball back down the hall, straight through an iron pillar and deep into Geirrod's stomach. After this, the thunder god laid about the frost giant's servants with the magic staff.

GERDA, in Germanic mythology, was a beautiful frost giantess and daughter of the giant Gymir, who reluctantly became the wife of FREYR, the fertility god. Although initially resistant to the idea, she was persuaded to marry by Freyr's faithful servant SKIRNIR, when he threatened to recite a terrible spell. This spell would have made Gerda so ugly than no man would ever come near her again. She would be transformed into "a sight to make the blood run cold". So it was that Gerda met Freyr in a forest after nine nights, representing the nine months of the northern winter. The Aurora Borealis was believed by some to be the radiance of Gerda. (See also TRAGIC LOVERS)

GINNUNGAGAP, in Germanic mythology, was a "yawning emptiness" at the time of creation, which lay between the realms of fire and cold. As the warm air from the south met the chill of the north, the ice of Ginnungagap melted and from the drops was formed *YMIR*, the frost giant, and *AUDHUMLA*, the primeval cow. By licking the ice, Audhumla uncovered *BURI*, ancestor of the gods. Buri's three grandsons, *ODIN*, *VILI* and *VE*, killed Ymir and took his body to the centre of Ginnungagap. There they made Midgard, the world of men, from his body. Ymir's flesh became the earth, his bones the mountains, his teeth rocks and stones, his hair the trees and his blood turned into the lakes and seas. The brothers used his skull to form the sky, with four dwarfs named Nordi, Sudri, Austri and Westri holding up the corners.

GJALP ("Howler") was a frost giantess, daughter of *GEIRROD*, who, along with her sister Greip, tried to kill *THOR*, the Germanic thunder god. When Thor, accompanied by the fire god *LOKI*, came to the hall of Geirrod, Gjalp did what she could to harm the visitors. Even before their arrival she added a torrent of her menstrual blood to a river in order to drown Thor and Loki. A well-aimed stone stopped Gjalp and sent her howling home. However, she and Greip then tried to ram the head of sleeping Thor against the rafters by suddenly raising his chair. The thunder god woke just in time to force the chair downwards by using a magic staff. Its massive weight broke the backs of the two giantesses and they died in agony on the floor.

GERDA (above), a frosty beauty, inspired the love of Freyr who sent Skirnir to win her hand. Although he offered her the apples of youth, and revealed his master's glowing portrait reflected in water, she remained unmoved until forced by threat of magic to consent. (ILLUSTRATION BY H THEAKER, C. 1920.)

GJALP (right) stirs up a river into a great flood, engulfing Thor as he wades across. Thor managed to stem the torrent by striking Gjalp with a boulder. He then heaved himself ashore by grasping a mountain ash named "Thor's Salvation". (ILLUSTRATION BY JAMES ALEXANDER, 1995.)

GINNUNGAGAP (right), the primal abyss at the dawn of creation, lay between the icy north and fiery south. Twelve swirling streams gushed into its vacuum and froze into massive ice blocks. In the south, fiery sparks slowly melted the ice, and from the icy droplets slowly emerged a frost giant. (ILLUSTRATION BY NICK BEALE, 1995.)

G

GRENDEL, a man-devouring monster, met his match in the fearless warrior Beowulf, who seized the creature's hairy limb in a vice-like grip and wrenched it from its socket. Howling with pain and rage, Grendel fled back to his watery lair and bled to death. (ILLUSTRATION BY ALAN LEE, 1984.)

GRENDEL was the name of a water monster which was invulnerable to weapons and troubled the kingdom of King Hrothgar of Denmark. One night Grendel, "grim and greedy, brutally cruel", came to the royal hall and ate a sleeping warrior, but a visiting warrior, BEOWULF, held one of the monster's arms in a vice-like grip. In the fierce struggle that ensued, Grendel's arm was torn off and he ran away and bled to death in his watery lair. It was in this lair that, later, Beowulf killed the monster's mother. Grendel's head was so large that when Beowulf brought it back as a trophy to King Hrothgar, he needed the assistance of four men to carry it.

GRID was a kindly frost giantess who helped the Germanic thunder god THOR in his struggle against GEIRROD. Thor had been lured by LOKI, the fire god, into danger without the protection of his magic belt of strength and his magic hammer. Grid loaned Thor her own belt, iron gloves and unbreakable staff to face Geirrod. In some traditions she is said to have borne ODIN a son, the silent god VIDAR, and to have made for him a special shoe which enabled him to stand in the mouth of the wolf FENRIR.

GRIMHILD see SORCERY AND SPELLS

GROA, according to Germanic mythology, was a seeress and the wife of Aurvandil, whose frozen toe THOR turned into a star by throwing it up into the sky. Exactly who this Aurvandil, or Aurvandill, was remains uncertain, though it has been suggested that he may have been a fertility god of the wetlands. Groa herself tried by magic to remove whetstone fragments from Thor's head after his fight with the frost giant HRUNGNIR. They had come from Hrungnir's sharp-edged, three-cornered stone when it had collided with Thor's hammer in mid-air. So excited was Groa, however, by Thor's news about the star and the return of her lost husband that she unfortunately failed to finish the spell, and this was why a few fragments of whetstone remained in Thor's head. Some time after her death, Groa was roused from the grave by her son, Svipdrag, who needed her advice on how he could win the love of the beautiful Menglad.

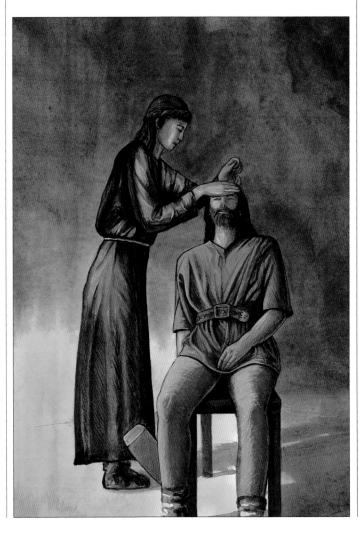

GUNGNIR was the magic spear belonging to ODIN, the leader of the Germanic gods. It was forged by dwarfs, the sons of Ivaldi, at the same time as a wig of spun gold, which the fire god LOKI ordered as a replacement for the golden hair of THOR's wife SIF. Mischievous Loki had cut off her beautiful locks as a joke. Having made the wig, the dwarfs decided to please the gods by using the furnace to make a ship for FREYR and, for Odin, a spear that managed to be both strong and slender, and never missed its mark. It was required in Viking custom that a spear should be thrown over the heads of an enemy before battle commenced, as an entreaty for Odin's aid. When the god hung himself on the cosmic tree YGGDRASIL for nine nights in order to obtain wisdom, he was, just like Christ, stabbed with a spear. (See also TREASURES AND TALISMANS)

GUDRUN see THE VALKYRIES

GUNNER see NORSE HEROES

HARBARD ("grey-beard"), in Germanic mythology, was a surly boatman. Wishing to cross a deep river, the god THOR summoned Harbard to ferry him over, only to be met by insults. Thor could think of no response to Harbard's abuse other than anger, but the boatman remained away from the bank. In his fury, Thor failed to notice that Harbard was his father ODIN. The meeting between the two gods reveals their different characters: Odin, the deceitful troublemaker and braggart; while Thor is hot-tempered but honest.

GROA, a gifted healer, chants charms over Thor in order to loosen the stone splinters lodged in the god's forehead. Feeling relief and gratitude, Thor rashly revealed that her long-lost husband was alive. The happy news so excited Groa that she forgot her spells and so left a splinter in Thor's head. (ILLUSTRATION BY NICK BEALE, 1995.)

GUNGNIR (above) was the name of Odin's spear; both slender and strong, it was unswerving in its flight. The weapon was so sacred that oaths were sworn on its point. Dvalin, the dwarf, forged its head, and Odin made the staff, carving it with magic runes. (ODIN BY R FOGELBERG, MARBLE, C. 1890.)

HEIMDALL

HEIMDALL, or Heimdalr, was the son of nine mothers and the watchman for the Germanic gods. Originally, he may have been an omniscient sky god. He could hear the sound of grass and wool growing, and see for over a hundred miles. He stood upon BIFROST, the three-strand bridge that linked ASGARD and Midgard (heaven and earth respectively). There he stood ready to blow his horn Gjall at the onset of RAGNAROK, during which he was to be the last to fall in single combat with LOKI. Heimdall's name may be related to the concept of a "world tree", as he was thought to be the supreme watchman perched at its top, above the highest rainbow. He disguised himself as RIG, the mortal who established the three social groups: the nobles, the peasants, and the enslaved. Disguised as Rig, the god visited in turn three houses in Midgard and fathered handsome children for the nobility, sturdy children for the peasants and ill-favoured children for the slaves.

HEIMDALR see HEIMDALL

HEIMDALL (right), bright guardian of the Bifrost Bridge, was ever alert, sleeping less than a bird. Gifted with special sight and hearing, he could see for 100 miles by night or day, and hear grass growing on the hillside. With his curved herald's horn, he would summon the gods to Ragnarok. (ILLUSTRATION BY NICK BEALE, 1995.)

GUNGNIR'S (below) spear shaft was carved from the sacred wood of Yggdrasil. After gaining wisdom at the World Tree, Odin broke off a bough, and fashioned a perfect staff from its holy wood. Here, the one-eyed, all-seeing god peers through the boughs of the sacred ash. (ILLUSTRATION BY ALAN LEE, 1984.)

TREASURES AND TALISMANS

THE MOST CELEBRATED CRAFTSMEN of the Norse world were wise and gifted dwarfs who laboured underground in caverns studded with gems. With superhuman artistry and secret wisdom, they fashioned fabulous treasures and talismans for gods and heroes. Some of their creations were exquisitely beautiful, such as the Brisingamen necklace; others were supernaturally powerful, such as the silken thread which fettered the fierce wolf, Fenrir. Most indispensable were the gods' wondrous weapons – Thor's boomerang hammer, Mjollnir, and Odin's infallible spear, Gungnir. The tireless dwarfs were also innovative engineers who crafted a collapsible, flying ship for Freyr and a sword that fought of its own accord once drawn. Most amazing of all, perhaps, were their living treasures, the gold-bristled boar, Gullinbursti, and Sif's golden hair which grew naturally. Some precious marvels were created by nature, such as the golden apples of youth. Among mortals, only Volund the smith could match the dwarfs in artistry and craft while, among sorcerers, the Finnish Ilmarinen excelled in magical craft and produced a peerless talisman, the Sampo.

IDUN'S (left) golden apples kept the gods eternally young. The fabulous fruit tree was tended and guarded by the three wise Norns who allowed only Idun, the deity of Spring, to pick the magic fruit. Yet such precious gifts were coveted by the giants who sought to strip the gods of their vigour and youth. Here, the giant Thiassi, disguised as a bird, carries Idun and her apples off in an ill-fated attempt to steal the gods' elixir of life. (ILLUSTRATION BY H THEAKER, C. 1920.)

THE BRISINGAMEN (above) necklace was crafted by four dwarfs with such artistry that it glittered like a constellation of stars in the night sky. Around Freyja's lovely neck it became an emblem of the fruits of the heavens and earth. She, in her turn, produced treasures for the earth whenever she cried, and Freyja wept profusely, especially during her search for her husband, Odur. When her tears fell on rock, they turned to gold, but tears shed at sea turned to amber. (FREYJA BY N J O BLOMMER, detail, canvas, 1852.)

MJOLLNIR (left), Thor's wondrous hammer, was never far from his grasp, as seen here in this characteristic pose of the god with his hammer clutched close to his heart. The Mjollnir was used as a fiery thunderbolt, launching shafts of lightning, and as a weapon for smashing giants' skulls. It was a talisman of both creativity and destruction, and was used to hallow both birth and death ceremonies. (BRONZE, 10TH CENTURY.)

GUNGNIR (right), Odin's great spear, never missed its mark. The spear shaft was fashioned by Odin from the sacred ash of Yggdrasil and carved with the god's magic runes. Just as valuable was Odin's fabulous ring, Draupnir, which produced eight similar gold rings every nine days, an everlasting source of wealth and power. (ILLUSTRATION BY H HENDRICH, C. 1906.)

THE SAMPO (below) was forged by Ilmarinen, the Eternal Hammerer of Finnish myth, who hammered out the sky at the dawn of time. Over three days, the talisman was fashioned mysteriously from one swift quill, milk of the fertile cow, a grain of barley and the fleece of a summer lamb. So out of the magical flames of the forge the Sampo was created; it consisted of a flour mill, salt mill and money mill, ensuring lasting prosperity and power. Here, the master smith looks intently into the furnace to see what the fire has produced. (THE FORGING OF THE SAMPO BY A GALLEN-KALLELA, CANVAS, C. 1852.)

WONDROUS LONGSHIPS (above) belonged to both Freyr and Thorstein. The god's ship, Skidbladnir, was crafted by the dwarfs. A personification of the clouds, it glided across land, sea and air. Although massive enough to convey all the gods and an entire host, it could be folded up and pocketed like a handkerchief. Thorstein's fabulous dragon boat, Ellida, was a gift from the sea god, Aegir. Shaped by swelling planks which grew together in the form of a winged dragon, Ellida raced with the whistling wind and outstripped the eagle. The floating fortress was famed far and wide. (ILLUSTRATION BY I J BILIBIN, C. 1900.)

HEL was the daughter of trickster *LOKI*, the fire god, and the frost giantess *ANGRBODA*. She was ruler of the Germanic netherworld (also called Hel), to which she had been banished by *ODIN*, the chief god. Once there, however, her powers were stronger than Odin's, for when Odin's son *BALDER* was killed Hel refused to return him to his parents. Her brothers, *FENRIR* the wolf and *JORMUNGAND* the serpent, were as terrifying as she, though it was Hel and her ghastly home which were adopted by the Christians as the name for their realm of eternal damnation.

The unpleasantness of Hel's realm stands in marked contrast to the pleasurable and enviable after-life that was enjoyed by the heroic dead who dwelt in Odin's wondrous hall *VALHALLA*. However, Hel's subjects were little more than silent attendants of the semi-decomposed queen. She was only partly decomposed because she had the face and body of a living woman, but her thighs and legs were those of a corpse. Hel's throne was known as the Sick Bed and her subjects were "all who died through sickness and old age".

HERMOD leaps bravely into misty Hel on his vain mission to seek Balder's release from death. The great noise made by the hero and his eight-hoofed horse Sleipnir when they crossed the crystal Gioll Bridge, provoked the grim guardian, Modgud, to complain irritably that Hermod must be alive. (ILLUSTRATION BY PETER HURD, 1882.)

HIMINBRIOTER see *HIMINRJOT*

HIMINRJOT, or Himinbrioter, ("Sky Bellower") was the head of a gigantic black ox. The ox belonged to *HYMIR* with whom *THOR* went fishing for *JORMUNGAND*, the sea serpent. Thor had no trouble in breaking Himinrjot's neck, despite

HEL, the grim goddess of the dead, listens unimpressed to Hermod's plea to release the much-loved god Balder from her dismal realm. Behind her, kneeling, there are rows of her sad subjects – souls of the old, sick or criminal who suffered ceaseless cold, pain and hunger in their cheerless, dreary home. (ILLUSTRATION BY JAMES ALEXANDER, 1995.)

HERMOD, in Germanic mythology, was the son of *ODIN* and *FRIGG*, and brother of *BALDER*. Rather like the Greek god Hermes and the Roman Mercury, he acted as a divine messenger. Hermod also shared these gods' interest in the dead, for it was he who was sent to *HEL* after Balder's death to ask for his brother's release. He rode there on Odin's famous horse, the eight-legged *SLEIPNIR*. When Hel refused to let Balder go until everything wept for him, Hermod was allowed to take back to *ASGARD* the arm-ring which Odin had fastened to Balder's body as a memento.

Hermod nearly met his own death on a journey to Midgard, the land of men. He was sent there by Odin to consult a Finn named Rossthiof about his worries concerning the future. He was saved by magic, however, and returned to reassure his father as best he could.

the animal's vast size, and used its head to bait his hook. Jormungand rose for this delicacy, but the head stuck in his throat. Thor would have landed the prize had not the sight of the serpent rising from the depths of the sea terrified Hymir. In the confusion that ensued Hymir was able to cut the great sea serpent free.

HOD see *HODR*

HODR, sometimes Hodur or Hod, the son of *ODIN* and *FRIGG*, was the blind god of Germanic mythology. In the Icelandic tradition, Hodr unintentionally killed his brother *BALDER*. When Balder was troubled by dreams of his coming death, his mother Frigg exacted a promise from each and every thing not to do her son any harm. A sole exception was the mistletoe, a plant the goddess considered to be too insignificant. The trickster

god *LOKI* learned about the mistletoe, however, and guided Hodr's hand when he threw it at his brother. The branch of mistletoe went straight through Balder, who fell down dead. Once it became clear that Balder would have to stay in the land of the dead, Hodr was sent to join him as a punishment. In a very different version of the story, Hodr and Balder are rivals for the hand of Nanna, and Balder is portrayed as a hateful figure. Their conflict is finally resolved when Hodr kills Balder with a magic sword. This Danish version shows the brothers in a very different light.

HERMOD (below) spurs his fabulous steed to assail the barred gate of Hel. Within, Balder can be seen waiting stoically beside an alarming creature, who is possibly one of the starved inmates of Hel. Balder, who knew the future well, knew that he was destined to remain in cheerless Hel for ever. (ILLUSTRATION FROM THE PROSE EDDA, 1760.)

HODR (above), who was blind from birth, unwittingly slew his beloved brother, Balder, prompted by the twisted god, Loki. Here, Loki gleefully guides Hodr's hand to aim a deadly dart of mistletoe at Balder, while the other gods look on in shocked dismay. (THE DEATH OF BALDER BY C ECKERSBERG, CANVAS, C. 1840.)

After *RAGNAROK*, the doom of the gods, "Balder and Hodr return from the world of the dead", reconciled, to a new earth. That these two sons of Odin are mentioned together here shows their importance in Icelandic mythology. First there is Balder, handsome and kind, almost too good for the world. He represents the positive side of his father's nature, as the god of magic and inspiration. The second brother, Hodr, is the opposite of Odin's foresight. Instead, he represents his blind spot, the side of his nature that takes delight in

death. Not for nothing was Balder slain by his blind brother in a game that involved throwing potentially dangerous objects.

HODUR see *HODR*

HOENIR see *HONIR*

HOGNI and his brother, Gunner, befriended the hero *SIGURD*, who owned a famous but ill-fated fortune generated by a magic ring called Andvarinaut. Under the ring's spell, Sigurd had unwittingly betrayed the Valkyrie *BRYNHILD*. She asked the brothers for help, and, bewitched by the curse, they arranged Sigurd's death. However, when Hogni and Gunner inherited Sigurd's fortune, they in turn were doomed and suffered at the hands of the Atli who coveted the gold. (See also *NORSE HEROES*)

HONIR, or Hoenir, according to Germanic mythology, was a member of the *AESIR* group of gods and brother of *ODIN*, the chief god. Apart from a terrible inability to make up his mind, his other prominent characteristic was said to be his long-leggedness. Sent to live among the *VANIR* as a token of goodwill after peace was agreed between the two warring branches of the gods, Honir unfortunately proved to be a grave disappointment to his new companions, who became increasingly angry at the way he appeared always to rely on his fellow Aesir, the wise *MIMIR*, when it came to making decisions of any kind. The Vanir therefore killed Mimir and sent his head back to the Aesir. In some versions of the Germanic creation story, it was believed that Honir was the god who gave humans their senses.

HOGNI (below) listens suspiciously to Brynhild's passionate plea for vengeance on her lover, Sigurd, who had unwittingly betrayed her love. Although refusing to kill Sigurd himself, he persuaded Guttorm to undertake the awful deed. Brynhild was later filled with remorse and killed herself. (ILLUSTRATION BY ARTHUR RACKHAM, C. 1900.)

HREIDMAR, or Reidmar, according to Germanic mythology, was a magician-farmer and the father of *REGIN*, *FAFNIR* and *OTTER*. When Otter, who was a shape-changer, was killed accidentally by *LOKI*, Hreidmar demanded to be compensated and told Loki to obtain enough gold to cover Otter's flayed skin, inside and out. The wily fire god seized the dwarf *ANDVARI*'s treasure, but the dwarf placed a curse upon it. Hreidmar was so pleased with the gold that he did not worry about the curse. But his second son, Fafnir, came to covet the treasure and killed him for it. Fafnir changed into a dragon to guard the gold and Regin asked *SIGURD* to slay him and recover the treasure, but he was killed as well.

HRUNGNIR, in Germanic mythology, was the strongest of the frost giants and owner of a powerful stallion named Gullfaxi, or Golden Mane. He encountered *ODIN* on one of the god's journeys through the nine worlds and challenged him to a horse race. Mounted on eight-legged *SLEIPNIR*, Odin won a narrow victory over Hrungnir on Golden Mane. By this time, the two had ridden to *ASGARD*, the divine stronghold, where Hrungnir was invited to rest before returning to *JOTUNHEIM*, the land of the giants. But Hrungnir drank too much strong ale and became arrogant. He even threatened to carry *VALHALLA*, the hall in which the honoured dead lived with Odin, off to Jotunheim on his back and to kill

HRUNGNIR (left), a mighty frost giant with a stony heart and skull, foolishly balances on his stone shield, believing that his expected foe, Thor, plans to attack him from below. Fully exposed to the impact of Thor's crushing hammer, the giant tries to deflect the hammer with his whetstone. (ILLUSTRATION BY JAMES ALEXANDER, 1995.)

HUGI (above) outstrips his rival Thialfi, an athletic warrior, competing in a contest of skills between gods and giants. Try as he would, Thialfi could not outrun his frosty rival who gathered speed at every step for, unknown to Thialfi, Hugi was an illusion symbolizing Thought, ever faster than action. (ILLUSTRATION BY JAMES ALEXANDER, 1995.)

all the gods, except *FREYJA* and *SIF*. At this point the giant-slayer *THOR* returned and waved his magic hammer at Hrungnir, but the frost giant, understanding that he would be easily killed without his own weapons, challenged Thor to a duel on the border between Asgard and Jotunheim. No one had met the thunder god in single combat before. Thor accepted eagerly, even though Hrungnir's head, heart and shield were made of stone.

When the frost giants heard about the forthcoming duel, they were both proud and anxious: proud that Hrungnir had challenged Thor, but anxious lest the god slay the most powerful of their number. So they made out of clay a man so huge that the thunder god would shake with fright when he first caught sight of him. The heart of a dead mare was used to animate the clay giant, whom they called Mist Calf. Alongside Mist Calf stood Hrungnir, awaiting the arrival of Thor. The frost giant knew that he had to avoid his opponent's hammer, and he held his sharp whetstone in readiness. As soon as Thor was in range, he hurled his magic weapon at Hrungnir, who swiftly launched his own sharp-edged, three-cornered stone in Thor's direction. The weapons met in mid-air. Although the hammer shattered the whetstone and went

on to crush Hrungnir's skull, a number of stone fragments lodged in Thor's head and he was also pinned beneath one of the fallen Hrungnir's legs. After this heroic incident, Thor became known as "Hrungnir's skull splitter".

HUGI ("Thought"), in Germanic mythology, was a young frost giant who outran THOR's human servant THIALFI in a race. The story of Thor's journey to the stronghold of UTGARD in the land of the frost giants is full of magic. The race between Hugi and Thialfi was but one incident in this strange adventure, which shows Thor to be an ineffectual strong man in the face of cunning spells. Throughout the journey the trickster LOKI, the god of fire, had cause to remind Thor of the superiority of brain over brawn. At one point Thor, Loki, Thialfi and his sister ROSKVA inadvertently slept in the thumb of an empty glove belonging to the enormous frost giant SKRYMIR, mistaking it for a vast hall. When he woke, Skrymir warned them that at Utgard there were giants even greater than he. Sure enough, when the travellers reached Utgard, they were unable to see the top of its battlements

without pressing the crowns of their heads on the napes of their necks. Inside the great fortress Thor and his companions failed in a number of tests, the thunder god himself being wrestled down on one knee by an "old, old woman". He also failed to empty a drinking horn, only to learn afterwards how its other end was in the sea. At the end of their adventure, however, the travellers saw that Skrymir and Utgard were no more than magic creations sent out by the frightened frost giants to mystify mighty Thor.

HUGINN ("Thought") and Muninn ("Memory") were the ravens of ODIN, the chief Germanic god. In order to be informed about events in the nine worlds, Odin sent the ravens out every day to see and hear all that happened there. They would then return to rest on Odin's shoulders and tell him what they had observed.

HYMIR ("Dark One") was a frost giant and, according to some traditions, father of the war god TYR. Hymir had an enormous cauldron, so deep that it could brew ale for all the gods. Without this huge vessel, there was no way that the sea god

AEGIR could offer hospitality to ODIN and his companions, so Tyr and THOR were sent to fetch it. When they arrived at Hymir's hall, Tyr's mother advised them to hide until she had explained their presence. Hymir found them and offered them a meal, though he felt uneasy. Thor astonished the assembled company by eating two whole oxen by himself. The next day their host suggested they go fishing if they wanted to eat again. Together they put to sea in Hymir's boat, Thor baiting his colossal hook with the head of HIMINRJOT, the giant's black ox. When the sea monster

HUGINN (left), one of Odin's fabulous ravens, whose name means Thought, was an airborne gatherer of news. Along with his brother raven, Muninn, or Memory, he flew through the nine worlds collecting information. They would then fly back to Odin and whisper the latest news into his ear. (ILLUSTRATION FROM THE PROSE EDDA, 1760.)

JORMUNGAND took this bait and Thor set about its head with his hammer, Hymir shook with terror. In the confusion Jormungand tore itself free of the great hook and sank bleeding beneath the surface of the waves. Two whales had to suffice for food instead.

Back in Hymir's hall, relations between host and guest quickly deteriorated into violence. Goblets were thrown before Thor left with the gigantic cauldron. When Hymir and some frost giants attempted to follow him in order to regain the cauldron, Thor used his hammer to such effect that all were killed.

HYMIR and Thor (below) forage for food on a fated fishing trip. Thor's tantalizing bait attracted the monstrous water serpent, Jormungand, which delighted the god who battled furiously with his giant catch. When the struggle threatened to capsize the boat, however, Hymir, in fear, cut the line. (ILLUSTRATION FROM THE PROSE EDDA, 1760.)

IDUN, Idunnor or Iduna, was, in Germanic mythology, the goddess who guarded the apples of youth. She was the wife of *BRAGI*, the god of poetry. When *LOKI*, the fire god, was captured by the frost giant *THIASSI*, he had to promise to steal the apples from Idun to secure his release. On his return to *ASGARD*, therefore, Loki told Idun that he had discovered apples of much better quality growing nearby, and so the goddess trustingly accompanied him into the forest, where, in the shape of an eagle, Thiassi awaited his prey. He took Idun and her apples in his claws and flew to *JOTUNHEIM*, the land of the frost giants. The loss of the apples at first caused the gods to become weak and old, with bleary eyes and loose

IDUN guarded a fabulous fruit tree, which produced life-giving apples. Here, she hands out her precious gifts to the ever-youthful gods from her inexhaustible casket. The mythic tradition of the golden apple, symbolizing immortality and fertility, can be found in both ancient Greek and Celtic cultures. (ILLUSTRATION BY J PENROSE, C. 1890.)

skin. Then their minds began to weaken, as a general fear of death settled on Asgard. At last *ODIN* gathered his remaining strength and found Loki. By threat of magic he compelled Loki to bring back Idun and her apples.

Loki flew to Jotunheim as a falcon, changed Idun into a nut and carried her home. The frost giant gave chase as an eagle, but he was burned to death by fires placed along the tops of Asgard's mighty walls. Loki then restored Idun to her true shape and she gave magic apples to the ailing gods. (See also *TREASURES AND TALISMANS*)

IDUNA see *IDUN*

JORMUNGAND (left), the serpent son of Loki, was hurled into the icy ocean by Odin. There he grew to such a monstrous size that he encircled Midgard and threatened sailors throughout the oceans. Here, the World Serpent rises to a bait of ox head, dangling from Thor's fishing line. (ILLUSTRATION FROM THE PROSE EDDA, 1760.)

JOTUNHEIM (right), the home of the frost giants, was a snow-covered wasteland on the ocean edge, possibly near the North Pole. It was a realm of mists, blizzards and roaring winds. From here the frost giants directed blasts of wind to nip the buds of spring. (ILLUSTRATION BY NICK BEALE, 1995.)

IDUNNOR see *IDUN*

INGEBORG see *TRAGIC LOVERS*

JEZI BABA see *BABA YAGA*

JORMUNGAND, in Germanic mythology, was the serpent son of *LOKI*, god of fire, and the frost giantess *ANGRBODA*, and brother of *FENRIR* and *HEL*. *ODIN* arranged for these monstrous children to be kidnapped and brought to *ASGARD*. He then threw Jormungand into the ocean, where he grew so long that he encircled the earth, and was known as the Midgard Serpent. At *RAGNAROK* Jormungand was to come on to the earth and be slain by *THOR*. (See also *RAGNAROK*)

JOTUNHEIM was the land given to the frost giants by *ODIN* and his brothers at the Creation. With its stronghold of *UTGARD*, it was one of the nine worlds sheltered by the cosmic tree *YGGDRASIL*. The others were *ASGARD*, the home of the *AESIR*, one branch of the gods; Vanaheim, the home of the *VANIR*, the other branch of the divine family; Alfheim, the land of the light elves; Nidavellir, the land of the dwarfs; Midgard, the home of humankind; Svartalfheim, the land of the dark elves; *HEL*, the realm of the unworthy dead; and cold Niflheim beneath Yggdrasil's roots. A mountainous region of freezing cold, Jotunheim was variously described as being inside Midgard, the land of mortals, or over the sea.

JUMALA was the creator god of Finnish mythology and their supreme deity. Very little is known about him, except that the oak tree was sacred to him. He was later replaced by Ukko, also a supreme god, but a deity of the sky and the air, who allowed the rain to fall. Ukko's wife was Akka, which suggests a link with *MADDER-AKKA*, the creator goddess of the Lapps.

KIED KIE JUBMEL was a stone god worshipped by the Lapps, the northernmost people of Europe. Reindeer were sacrificed to Kied Kie Jubmel as late as the seventeenth century to ensure success in the hunt. He seems to have been regarded as "lord of the herds". Among the Swedes he was known as Storjunka, or "Great Lord".

KREIMHILD see *TRAGIC LOVERS*

LEMINKAINEN (above) was slain and dismembered during one of his exploits. But his magician mother gathered him up and restored him to life. Here she calls upon a bee to bring life-giving honey from beyond the highest heaven. (LEMINKAINEN'S MOTHER BY A GALLEN-KALLELA, CANVAS, C.1890.)

KULLERVO see *SORCERY AND SPELLS*

KVASIR

KVASIR was a wise man in Germanic mythology. His name means "spittle" and recalls his creation when the gods spat into a jar to mark the end of conflict between two branches of the divine family, the *VANIR* and the *AESIR*. The Aesir then took the jar and Kvasir was made from the spittle. Renowned for his great wisdom, he travelled the world and wherever he went people stopped what they were doing to listen to him. He was killed by two dwarfs, *FJALAR* and Galar, who wanted his wisdom. They mixed his blood with honey in order to make a wonderful mead which gave the gift of poetry to everyone who drank it.

LEIB-OLMAI

LEIB-OLMAI ("Alder man") was a Lapp bear god. At bear festivals hunters used to sprinkle their faces with an extract of alder bark. As the protector of bears, Leib-Olmai required certain prayers before he would allow any man to kill a bear.

LEMINKAINEN

LEMINKAINEN ("Lover") was one of the heroes of Finnish epic. As a child, he was bathed by his mother three times in one summer night and nine times in one autumn night to ensure that he would become a wise adult, gifted

KVASIR (right), a character endowed with wondrous wisdom, was created from the spittle of the gods. He travelled the world inspiring gods and mortals with his sense and wisdom. After his death his blood was used to make a mead of inspiration. (ILLUSTRATION FROM THE PROSE EDDA, 1760.)

with a talent for song. A carefree young man, many of his adventures involve the pursuit of women and he accompanied *VAINAMOINEN* on a journey to the land of Pohja in search of wives. His most dangerous exploit was an attempt to kill the swan of *TUONI*, the god of the dead. Failing to protect himself with magic, he was torn apart by Tuoni's son and his remains were scattered in the river. But his magician mother put his body back together again and restored him to life. (See also *NORSE HEROES*)

NORSE HEROES

THE VIKINGS were famed for their fighting spirit, facing death and doom with vigour and courage. Their hardy heroism was doubtless shaped by the crushing Nordic climate, but also by a stoic fatalism. While accepting the inevitability of death on the field and doom at the end of the world, the Norsemen fought with undiminished spirit. For the Vikings, word-fame was everything, redeeming and surviving a hero's death. After death, the bravest heroes went to Valhalla where they awaited the fated and fatal showdown at Ragnarok. No less than the heroes, the Norse gods were heroic, facing doom at Ragnarok with fighting spirit. Finnish heroes were quite as determined and brave in their way, though perhaps less grand and stoic. Armed with magical forces, they battled with incantations rather than force of arms. For the Finns, death was not always final: Leminkainen had more than one life, while aged Vainamoinen could always slip out of a tight corner by shifting shape.

GUNNER AND HOGNI (left), the Nibelung brothers, died gallantly though neither lived a flawless life. Drawn into the web of tragedy woven by a cursed ring, they slew the peerless hero Sigurd, and hoarded his gold. When seized by Atli, who coveted their gold, they refused to surrender under threat of death. Hogni died laughing as his heart was cut out; and Gunner, here, cast into a serpent's pit with bound hands, played his harp with his feet, defying death to the last. (WOOD CARVING, 12TH CENT.)

THOR (right), supernaturally strong and armed with the magical Mjollnir, was a formidable foe. Being neither immortal nor invulnerable, he fought with a fearless spirit, slaying giants with effortless ease and reckless rage. Along with some of the other gods, Thor was destined to die heroically at Ragnarok, after putting up a fierce fight and slaying his arch-foe, the World Serpent. (THOR AND THE GIANTS BY M E WINGE, CANVAS, DETAIL, C. 1890.)

SIGURD (above), the most famous of Iceland's heroes, slew the terrible dragon, Fafnir. Armed with his father's invincible sword, Sigurd hid in a hole in the dragon's slime track and, as Fafnir slithered across on his daily trip to the foul forest pool, thrust his sword into its belly. The bloated creature had grown increasingly monstrous in shape and character; all the better to guard his cursed treasure. Although Sigurd's heroic deed won him fame and fortune, his life from then on was blighted by the curse that came with the ill-fated treasure. (ILLUSTRATION BY ALAN LEE, 1984.)

SIGMUND THE VOLSUNG (right) proved his heroic status by drawing forth a magical sword thrust into the Branstock oak by Odin. With this sword he won fame throughout Scandinavia, but also provoked the envy of his brother-in-law, Siggeir, who resolved to slay all the Volsungs. All ten sons were tied to forest trees, prey to the beasts of the forest. Only Sigmund escaped, by biting off a wolf's tongue, and sought vengeance for his kinsmen. (ILLUSTRATION BY P WILSON, C. 1900.)

L

LESHY (left), spirit of the forest, though he appeared in the shape of a man, cast no shadow where he walked and could easily camouflage himself among his forest trees, sometimes as small as a leaf, sometimes as tall as the tallest tree. A jealous guardian of his leafy realm, he loved to lead trespassers astray. (ILLUSTRATION BY M VON SCHWIND, C. 1860.)

LIF (right) and her mate, Lifthrasir, took shelter at the end of the world in the sunlit branches of the cosmic ash tree, Yggdrasil. After the earth had been purged by fire and flood, the young couple climbed down and a new age dawned, a fresh green age in which they were destined to repopulate the world and so renew the human race. (ILLUSTRATION BY NICK BEALE, 1995.)

THE LESHY, also known as Lesovik and Lesiye, was the Slavonic spirit of the forest who led travellers and hunters astray in the woods. Although human in form, he had a long green beard and cast no shadow. His chief attribute, however, was his ability to change size: he could become as small as a mouse or as tall as the highest tree. Every October the Leshy went into a kind of hibernation, disappearing from his woodland home until the following spring, when he would return wilder and noisier than ever.

LESIYE see THE LESHY

LESOVIK see THE LESHY

LIF and Lifthrasir ("Life" and "Eager for Life") were the man and woman who were to hide in the cosmic ash tree YGGDRASIL at RAGNAROK, the doom of the gods. They were destined to survive this catastrophe and then repopulate a new world, which would rise from the sea like a volcanic island. "The bellowing fire will not scorch them; it will not even touch them, and their food will be the morning dew. Through the branches they will see a new sun burn as the world ends and starts again."

LIFTHRASIR see LIF

LODDFAFNIR, in Germanic mythology, was a man who learned the wisdom of the gods. He visited the Well of URD, where the gods held their daily assembly, and stayed in VALHALLA, ODIN's hall. His myth comprises a retelling of the knowledge he gathered there. It is an interesting mixture of commonsensical advice about good conduct and superstitions concerning the avoidance of witchcraft.

LOKI, sometimes Lopt, was the Germanic fire god and son of the giants FARBAUTI and Laufey. He was a mischief-maker, trickster and shape-changer, and grew progressively more evil until eventually the gods bound him in a cave until the coming of RAGNAROK, the end of the world. Boredom was a problem for Loki, who "was tired of the string of days that unwound without a knot or a twist in them".

The fact that his parents were giants may help to explain his tendency towards evil deeds. He

LOKI helped to precipitate a cycle of violence by callously slaying Otter for his fur. To appease Otter's father, Loki stole a dwarf's treasure, invoking his bitter curse. Here, Loki helps Odin quieten the raging dwarf, while at the top, Otter's brothers see a weeping Norn, which was an omen of doom. (ILLUSTRATION BY F VON STASSEN, 1914.)

simply could not help playing tricks and exposing the gods to danger, although it was often his quick-wittedness that afterwards saved them. Loki, for instance, brought about the loss and return of IDUN and her apples of youth. Without these magic fruit, the gods were subject to the ravages of time like everyone else. On occasion Loki was even prepared to risk serious harm to his companion THOR, the thunder god. When Loki led Thor unarmed to the hall of the frost giant GEIRROD, only the loan of weapons from the kindly frost giantess GRID saved the thunder god. Loki tricked his friend because the price of his own release by Geirrod had been delivery of the thunder god into his power.

Yet it was Loki who devised the novel scheme to get back Thor's magic hammer after it was stolen by dwarfs and passed into the hands of the frost giant THRYM. The price for the hammer's return, Loki discovered, was the hand of FREYJA, the fertility goddess. He therefore persuaded Thor to go to Thrym dressed in Freyja's clothes. When Thrym took out the magic hammer, Thor seized it and laid low all the frost giants present.

Loki was married twice, first to the giant ANGRBODA and then to SIGYN, with whom he had two sons, VALI and Narvi. His monstrous children by Angrboda were FENRIR, JORMUNGAND and HEL, ruler of the underworld: all fearsome representatives of the evil side of his nature. Even after he brought about the death of ODIN's son BALDER, the gods continued to tolerate his presence in ASGARD. But when he arrived at AEGIR's feast and began to torment everybody present with insults and sneers, their patience came to an end.

To escape their wrath Loki changed himself into a salmon. From his high seat in Asgard, however, Odin located the fish and mounted an expedition to catch it. Loki was then placed in a dark cave. His son Vali was changed into a wolf, who immediately attacked his brother Narvi and killed him. Narvi's intestines were then used to bind Loki beneath the dripping mouth of a venomous snake. In this dreadful prison, the god awaited Ragnarok. Then he was to emerge to lead the army of evil in their final battle with the gods, when Loki would meet his own end at the hands of HEIMDALL. (See also RAGNAROK)

LOPT see LOKI

LUONNOTAR (which probably means "Daughter of Nature") was the creator goddess of the Finns. At the beginning there was only Luonnotar "all alone in a vast emptiness". Later she floated for centuries on the cosmic ocean, until one day a bird made a nest on her knees and began to hatch some eggs. But the goddess became excited and upset the nest, with the result that from the broken shells of the eggs the heavens and the earth were formed. The yolks became the sun, and the whites the moon. Scattered fragments of these eggs were transformed into the stars. Afterwards Luonnotar fashioned the continents and the seas, and gave birth to VAINAMOINEN, the Finnish hero.

MADDER-AKKA and her male companion Madder-Atcha were, according to the Lapps, the divine couple who created humankind. Madder-Atcha was responsible for the soul and Madder-Akka for the body. The child they made was then placed in the womb of its earthly mother. Their three daughters were involved with procreation as well. Sarakka supported women during childbirth; if a male child was to be born, Juksakka ensured that the baby changed from its originally female gender, while Uksakka, who lived underground, looked after the interests of the new-born child. See also JUMALA.

LOKI (above), the trickster god, was at first just a playful prankster, but became so dark and twisted that the gods realized he was evil and resolved to imprison him. Loki was eventually bound to a rock, with his face exposed to the fiery drops of a snake's venom. (ILLUSTRATION BY D PENROSE, C. 1870.)

LUONNOTAR (below), a primal goddess, grew restless in the heavens and slipped into the cosmic sea, where she drifted until an eagle built a nest on her knee. When she accidentally upset the nest, its eggs broke and formed the earth and sky, sun, moon and stars. (ILLUSTRATION BY NICK BEALE, 1995.)

MAGNI ("Mighty") was the son of *THOR*, the Germanic thunder god, and the giantess Jarnsaxa, and brother of Modi. After his duel with *HRUNGNIR*, the strongest of the frost giants, Thor fell wounded to the ground, as fragments of whetstone had lodged in his head. He was also unable to move because one of Hrungnir's lifeless legs pinned him to the ground. Even worse, Thor wetted himself when he noticed the clay giant Mist Calf. Insult was nearly added to injury when, at the age of three years, Magni proved strong enough to free his father Thor, even though none of the gods had been able to shift Hrungnir's leg. "It's a pity I didn't come sooner," Magni commented. "If I had met this giant first, he would be fallen to my bare fists." Although *ODIN* was rather put out by young Magni's intervention, Thor showed his gratitude by giving the young frost giant Hrungnir's magnificent horse, Golden Mane. After *RAGNAROK*, the doom of the gods, Magni and Modi together would inherit Thor's magic hammer, *MJOLLNIR*.

MATI SYRA ZEMLYA ("Moist Earth Mother") was the Slavonic earth goddess. Archaeological evidence suggests that her worship may have originated in the basin of the River Don as much as 30,000 years ago. Believed to possess the ability to predict the future and to settle disputes wisely, she was an object of veneration up to the early years of the twentieth century, when Russian peasant women were still performing elaborate rites in order to summon her presence to protect them from disease.

MENU, or Menulis, was the Baltic moon god. The sun was imagined as the goddess *SAULE*, the patroness of green snakes. The Letts believed that the stars were the children of Menu and Saule. The Morning Star, however, was said to have been the child of a love affair between Saule and *PERKUNO*, the thunder god. For this reason the moon god, in shame and anger, avoided his spouse, and appeared only by night, while the sun goddess was happy to be seen all through the day.

MAGNI and his brother, Modi, stride across the sunlit Plain of Ida at the dawn of a fresh green age, after the world destruction of Ragnarok. Magni ("Mighty") swings Thor's sacred hammer, while Modi ("Courage") follows behind. (ILLUSTRATION BY JAMES ALEXANDER, 1995.)

MATI SYRA ZEMLYA was invoked by Slavic farmers at harvest time. They entered their fields at dawn and blessed the earth with libations of hemp oil. Bowing to the east, west, north and south, they invoked the primal deity, each time soaking the earth with oil. (ILLUSTRATION BY NICK BEALE, 1995.)

MENULIS see *MENU*

MIMIR, in Germanic mythology, was a wise god sent by the *AESIR* to the *VANIR* in order to seal the peace after these two branches of the divine family tired of war. Because the Vanir felt that they had been cheated, they cut off Mimir's head and sent it back to the Aesir. *ODIN*, however, smeared the severed head with herbs so that it would never rot. He then recited a charm over it to restore its power of speech. Later, Mimir's head was placed by Odin to guard a magic well under the root of the cosmic tree *YGGDRASIL*. To gain Mimir's wisdom, which comprised "many truths unknown to any other person", Odin gave one of his eyes for permission to drink at the well.

MJOLLNIR was the magic hammer of the Germanic thunder god *THOR*. Made by the dwarfs Brokk and Eitri, it was an instrument of destruction, fertility and resurrection. In Thor's hands Mjollnir was the gods' certain protection against their enemies, the frost giants. That is why the gods were so worried when the frost giant *THRYM* stole it. The price for its return was the hand of *FREYJA*, the fertility goddess. Dressed in Freyja's clothes and accompanied by the trickster god *LOKI*, Thor went to Thrym's hall. Since it was customary to ask a blessing on any marriage by placing the hammer on the knees of the bride, Thrym ordered it to be brought out. But no sooner had Thor got hold of Mjollnir than he jumped up and crushed the frost giant's skull with a mighty blow.

Mjollnir's powers as a restorer of life were revealed on a journey made by Thor to the frost giants' stronghold of *UTGARD*, when he used it to reconstitute from skin and bones two goats which had been eaten the night before. The magic hammer was also used at funerals. When the fire was lit round the pyre of *BALDER* and

MIMIR serves Odin a draught from his wondrous Fountain of Wisdom. The price demanded for this privilege was one eye, symbolizing the sacrifice of one view for another, greater vision. Odin's eye floated in the fountain, a symbol of the full moon, beside the crescent moon of Heimdall's horn. (ILLUSTRATION BY NICK BEALE, 1995.)

Nanna, Thor raised his hammer and chanted certain magic words to consecrate the ceremony.

After *RAGNAROK*, the day of doom and the end of the world, ownership of Mjollnir passed to Thor's sons *MAGNI* and Modi. (See also *TREASURES AND TALISMANS*)

MOKKURALFI, or Mist Calf, was a gigantic clay giant. He was made from the clay bed of a river by frost giants in order to terrify *THOR*, the thunder god. This occurred just before Thor met *HRUNGNIR*, the strongest of the frost giants, in single combat. Mist Calf was animated by the heart of a mare, but it proved inadequate for the task. Though the creature towered into the clouds, it was very slow-moving

and its legs were vulnerable to attack. On the day of the duel, Thor killed Hrungnir but wet himself at the sight of Mist Calf. His human servant *THIALFI* was less impressed, however, and swung his axe at the clay giant's legs. When Mist Calf toppled backwards, his fall shook *JOTUNHEIM*, the land of the frost giants.

MUNDILFARI was a man who offended *ODIN*. When Odin, along with his brothers *VILI* and *VE*, carved the world out of the carcass of *YMIR*, the original frost giant, they solved the problem of its illumination by using sparks and glowing embers from the sun, moon and stars. Mundilfari, who lived in Midgard, had a son and a daughter so handsome and beautiful that he called one Moon and the other Sun. The gods were angered by this comparison. Odin snatched the brother and sister from Midgard and turned them into constellations to guide the real heavenly bodies on their daily and nightly journeys across the sky.

MJOLLNIR (left), symbolizing Thor's thunderbolt, glowed red-hot at the mallet end, and could only be held by an iron gauntlet. It was not just destructive, but also creative and hallowed weddings and births. The exquisite, whirling patterns of Viking art beautifully depict the blazing eyes of the god. (SILVER PENDANT, 10TH CENTURY.)

MUNDILFARI (below) named his lovely children after the sun and moon, angering the gods with his arrogance. The children were made to drive the heavenly chariots across the sky. At left, the moon is drawn by All-Swift, while two eager steeds, Early Waker and Rapid Goer, pull the larger sun chariot. (ILLUSTRATION BY GLENN STEWARD, 1995.)

N

MYESYATS was the moon deity of Slavonic myth. Some traditions represent him as the cold, bald-headed uncle of the sun god *DAZHBOG*. In others, Myesyats is a beautiful woman, the consort of Dazhbog and mother by him of the stars. Every spring the divine pair are remarried, but in the autumn Dazhbog leaves his bride and only returns to her after the cold winter months have passed.

NERTHUS was a Germanic goddess, whose cult was described by the Roman writer Tacitus in the first century AD. According to him, she was an important mother goddess who had a sacred grove on a Frisian island. At regular intervals Nerthus travelled inland along a recognized route, her image placed in an ox cart and attended by a priest. During these sacred journeys peace was expected to prevail because "all iron was put away". At a certain lake the goddess bathed,

NERTHUS rides in a triumphal procession, during her biannual fertility festival. Bedecked with flowers, her chariot was drawn by two heifers, which symbolized primal motherhood and abundance. The people honoured her by laying aside all iron tools and weapons and donning festive dress. (ILLUSTRATION BY JAMES ALEXANDER, 1995.)

and afterwards slaves who had helped in this ritual were drowned in Nerthus' honour. Sacrifice by drowning was a practice also favoured by the ancient Slavs in eastern Europe. The name of the goddess may have meant "power-ful one" because it refers to strength. Quite possibly Tacitus was describing a local cult of *FREYJA*. Some versions of the myths of *ASGARD*, home of the gods, sug-gest that Nerthus was sister and wife to *NJORD*, the sea god, and mother of Freyja and *FREYR*.

NIDHOGG, in Germanic myth-ology, was the dragon living at one of the three roots of the cosmic tree *YGGDRASIL*. The freezing mist and darkness of Niflheim, which was the lowest of the nine worlds, was

NIDHOGG (left), a gruesome dragon, dwelt in icy Niflheim and, when not devouring corpses, it habitually nibbled the root of Yggdrasil, the cosmic tree. Here, a stag browsing on the leaves of Yggdrasil is in its turn nipped by Nidhogg, reflecting the life and death struggle at the root of the universe. (WOOD CARVING, 8TH CENTURY.)

where the dragon lived, ripping corpses apart and eating them. Between mouthfuls he would send the squirrel Ratatosk up the cosmic tree on an errand of insult, for the agile animal periodically disturbed two birds, an eagle and a hawk, who were perched at the very top. When momentarily tired of the taste of dead flesh, Nidhogg would gnaw at the root of Yggdrasil itself, presumably hoping to inflict dam-age on the cosmos in some way. Both Yggdrasil and Nidhogg were destined to survive the final cata-strophe of *RAGNAROK*, the doom of the gods and the end of the world. Neither fire nor flood could deter the dragon from its ceaseless feast-ing on the vast and inexhaustible supply of dead.

NJORD was the Germanic sea god, a member of the divine race of *VANIR* and father of the fertility gods *FREYR* and *FREYJA*. When peace was agreed between the *AESIR* and the Vanir, the two branches of the divine family, Njord, Freyr and Freyja came to live with the Aesir as a sign of goodwill. According to some versions of the myth, the mother of Freyr and Freyja was Njord's own sister *NERTHUS*, but

NJORD (below) lines up with the gods to have his feet inspected by Skadi, who was obliged to choose a husband from the shape of his feet. When Skadi picked Njord, she found that she had won a sweet, old sea god with passions quite opposite to her own, and so she soon took to her chilly hills alone. (ILLUSTRATION BY J HUARD, 1930.)

NJORD calmed the storms raised by the tempestuous god, Aegir. A gentle soul, Njord loved his sunlit coves and creeks, home of his sacred seagulls and swans. Popular with sailors and fishermen, he aided ships in distress, blew favourable winds and caused summer showers. (ILLUSTRATION BY JAMES ALEXANDER, 1995.)

since the Aesir disapproved of marriage between brother and sister, Nerthus did not accompany her husband and children to Asgard.

Njord's second marriage was to the frost giantess *SKADI*, who chose him on the basis of his beautiful feet. However, the couple could not agree about where they should live. Njord found Skadi's home in *JOTUNHEIM*, the land of the frost giants, too cold and barren, while Skadi disliked the noise and bustle of shipbuilding around Njord's hall of Noatun in Asgard. After nine nights in each place they decided to live apart. Skadi went back to her favourite pastime of hunting on skis and the weather-beaten Njord returned to a life at sea. The apparently unbridgeable gap between them probably reflects more than personal taste. Njord was certainly seen as a god of fertility, since he provided to those who worshipped him not only safe voyages at sea, but also wealth and good fortune in the form of land and sons. Skadi's associations were quite different, however. She came from a range of frozen mountains, where heavy clouds masked the sun and harsh rocks made the ground as barren as death. In her wild and unforgiving land, where nothing was able to grow or prosper at all, there was hardly any scope for humankind.

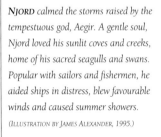

NORNIR see THE NORNS

THE NORNS, also known as the Nordic Fates, decided the destinies of both gods and mortals as they wove the Web of Fate. Here, at left, wise old Urd reads from the scroll of the past, while young Verdandi symbolizes the present, and veiled Skuld clasps her closed scroll of the future. (ILLUSTRATION BY JAMES ALEXANDER, 1995.)

THE NORNS, or Nornir, were the Germanic fates, the goddesses of destiny. The original Norn was undoubtedly *URD* ("Fate"). The Well of Urd, which was situated under one of the roots of the great cosmic tree *YGGDRASIL*, was the site where the gods held their daily assembly. The two other Norns known by name are Verdandi ("Present") and Skuld ("Future"). It was believed that the Norns decided the destinies of gods, giants and dwarfs, as well as of humankind. The Anglo-Saxons called Urd by the name of Wyrd, and in England there was maintained a belief in the tremendous powers of the three sisters long after the arrival of Christianity. For instance, in Shakespeare's tragic play *Macbeth*, the Three Sisters on "the blasted heath" obviously owed something to the Norns.

A clear parallel of the Norns are the Moerae, or "Fates", encountered in Greek mythology. As in the Germanic mythic tradition, they were seen as three sister goddesses: Klotho ("The Spinner"), Lachesis ("The Decider") and Atropos ("The Inevitable"). It would seem more than possible that the Norns were also originally thought of as spinners. However, in Germanic mythology the Greek and Roman concept of the Fates spinning an individual length of yarn for each mortal life does not appear.

THE VALKYRIES

VALKYRIES WERE ORIGINALLY SINISTER SPIRITS of slaughter, dark angels of death who soared over the battlefields like birds of prey, meting out fate in the name of Odin. Chosen heroes were gathered up and borne away to Valhalla, the heavenly abode of Odin's ghostly army. In later Norse myth, the Valkyries were romanticized as Odin's shield-maidens, virgins with golden hair and snowy arms who served the chosen heroes everlasting mead and meat in the great hall of Valhalla. On the battlefield, they soared over the host as lovely swan-maidens or splendid mounted Amazons. This far more appealing portrayal was further developed in the Volsung Saga and *Niebelungenlied*, where the heroine, Brynhild or Brunhild, was a beautiful, fallen Valkyrie. Idealized Valkyries were infinitely more vulnerable than their fierce predecessors, and often fell in love with mortal heroes. Swan-maidens, especially, were at risk as they might easily be trapped on earth if caught without their plumage.

MOUNTED VALKYRIES (left) soared over the battlefield through storm clouds on flying steeds. Their pearly mounts personified the rain clouds, spraying dew and hoar frost over a thirsty earth. The flying Amazon, here, expresses the swift, irrevocable force of fate and the finality of death. (THE VALKYRIE BY STEPHEN SINDRING, MARBLE, C. 1900.)

VALKYRIES (left) were originally demons of death who ravaged the battlefields or stormy seas, weaving the web of war, like the bloodthirsty Morrigu of Celtic myth. Behind the grisly image lay the ghastly necessity of death and revenge. The Valkyries' grim mission was reflected in their menacing names, such as Shrieking, Screaming or Raging. This striking modern portrayal captures the ancient vision of the Valkyries as wild and gleeful spirits of disorder and destruction, astride bat-like dragons. (THE RIDE OF THE VALKYRIES BY KARL ENGEL, CANVAS, C. 1860.)

ODIN (above) commanded the Valkyries, who dispatched his will on the battlefield without question. In a unique case of rebellion, the heroic Valkyrie, Brynhild, defied Odin by helping her half-brother, Siegmund, against his will. In penance, Brynhild was condemned to lie defenceless on a hilltop until claimed by a mortal. Later the god relented and softened his punishment by putting Brynhild to sleep in a ring of fire, protected against all but the bravest hero. (ODIN AND BRUNHILD BY F LEEKE, CANVAS, C. 1890.)

GUDRUN (above) fell in love with a mortal hero, Helgi. When Helgi died, Gudrun wept so much that he called from his grave, imploring her to stop crying, for each tear she shed so his wounds flowed. Soon after, Helgi's spirit rose to Valhalla where the lovers dwelt. Here, Gudrun gathers up the slain to swell the ghostly army which Helgi led at Ragnarok. (ILLUSTRATION BY K DIELITZ, C. 1890.)

A SERVING VALKYRIE (above) holds out a horn of plenty to welcome the chosen heroes to Valhalla. By the sixth century, the Valkyries were already being portrayed in a softer light as helpful handmaidens of Odin, gathering up the slain and serving the heroes in Valhalla. Clad in flowing robes and with long golden hair caught up in a bun, this gracious maiden helpfully offers a brimming horn of mead – a welcome sight for the weary warrior. (SILVER GILT, PENDANT, 6TH CENTURY.)

VALHALLA, (left), the glittering and magnificent Hall of the Slain in Asgard, the home of the gods, was built to house Odin's huge army of heroes who were gathered to fight at Ragnarok, the preordained doom of the gods. A Viking's paradise in every way, the splendid hall gleamed with walls of polished spears and vaults of shining shields. At the long benches, decorated with glowing chain mail, warriors wined and dined everyday on ever-flowing mead and everlasting meat, served by the lovely Valkyries. The heroic host, which was amassed over the centuries, must have been massive; to feed such an army the cook, Andhrimnir, stirred a mighty cauldron, called Eldhrimnir, in which he prepared an inexhaustible boar stew. (VALHALLA BY MAX BRUCKNER, CANVAS, 1896.)

O

ODIN, also known as Woden or Wotan, was the chief god of Germanic mythology, the son of *BOR* and grandson of *BURI*. He was particularly favoured by the Vikings and rose to prominence in the eighth and ninth centuries. These seafarers and raiders were attracted by Odin's love of battle as the "father of the slain", for in *VALHALLA*, an immense hall in the divine fortress of *ASGARD*, the one-eyed god was said to preside over the *EINHERJAR* ("glorious dead"). At this period it seems that Odin displaced *TYR*, whom the Romans had identified as the sky god of the north European peoples. Tyr retained his interest in war, but

Odin was looked upon as the inspiration for hard-bitten warriors. He alone had the power to inspire men in battle to a state of berserk rage in which they feared nothing and felt no pain. The terrible berserkers would rush naked into the fray, biting the edges of their shields in a maddened frenzy. Odin's name means something akin to "fury" or

ODIN (left), the highest of gods, sits on his exalted throne, Hlidskialf, which was a mighty watch-tower overlooking the nine worlds. Hovering nearby are his tireless ravens, the airborne news reporters, Huginn and Muninn, while at his feet crouch his pet wolves, Geri and Freki, omens of good luck. (ODIN BY E BURNE-JONES, C. 1870.)

"madness". It indicates possession, as in the battle-frenzy exhibited by the Irish hero Cuchulainn.

That Odin became the foremost god shows how important warfare always was in Germanic tradition. It should be noted, however, that he did not embody martial ecstasy himself; rather he inspired it in a devious manner. Odin was ever

ODIN (below), as the Wild Huntsman, leads the heroic host on a ghostly hunt through the stormy midnight sky. In the roar and rumble of the storm clouds, Norsemen fancied they heard Odin's phantom riders sweep across the sky, dark omens of doom. (THE WILD HUNT OF ODIN, BY P N ARBO, CANVAS, 1872.)

ready to stir up strife, and on one occasion commanded the fertility goddess FREYJA to "find two kings and set them at each other's throats" so that their vassals would wade through torrents of blood on the battlefield. The Danish King Harald was supposed to have been instructed in tactics by the god and granted many victories. In his final battle, though, Odin took the place of the king's charioteer and drove Harald to his death. When asked about such withdrawals of luck, Odin used to reply that "the grey wolf watches the halls of the gods". Gathering to Valhalla heroic warriors slain in battle was the only policy he could adopt under the constant threat of RAGNAROK, the doom of the gods. These Einherjar were desperately needed for the final battle on the VIGRID Plain, where nearly all would fall in a struggle between the gods and the frost giants. Odin himself was to be killed by the wolf FENRIR, the monstrous offspring of the fire god LOKI and the frost giantess ANGRBODA.

Besides his authority over the battlefield and the glorious dead, Odin was a god of magic and wisdom. As the oldest of the gods, the first-born son of Bor, he was treated by the other gods as their father. Shifty-eyed and flaming-eyed he might be, but Odin also had a strongly positive side to his character as the most learned god. His conflicting negative and positive aspects are indeed very similar to those of the Hindu god Shiva, the great destroyer-saviour of Indian mythology. For Odin's love of wisdom was so profound that he was prepared to sacrifice himself to plumb its depths. Odin was often portrayed as a grey-bearded old man with one eye, his face hidden by a hood or a broad-brimmed hat, because he had cast an eye into MIMIR's well in return for a drink of its "immense wisdom". He gained insight in another way by hanging himself for nine days from YGGDRASIL, the cosmic tree. This

voluntary death, and his subsequent resurrection by means of magic, gave Odin greater wisdom than anyone else.

It is possible that the obvious parallel between this myth and the Crucifixion gave Christianity a head-start in northern Europe. Odin's own worship appears to have gone into decline in the early eleventh century, at the close of the Viking age. Violent times were passing as Viking colonists settled down as peaceful farmers and traders. But during the Vikings'

ODIN (below), in a timeless battle scene, clasps his wife longingly, before diving into the fray. Armed for battle in eagle helmet and blue tunic, symbolizing the sky, he is armed with his infallible spear, Gungnir, and his wondrous ring Draupnir, which was the symbol of his power and wealth. (ODIN'S LEAVE-TAKING BY F LEEKE, CANVAS, C. 1875.)

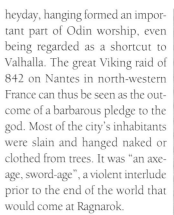

ODIN (above), a god of vision, sacrificed one eye for a draught of Mimir's Fountain of Wisdom. His single eye symbolized the radiant all-seeing sun, while his lost eye, floating in Mimir's well, signified the full moon. Odin hung himself from Yggdrasil, the cosmic tree for nine days, to learn the secrets of the dead. (BRONZE RELIEF, C. 1950.)

heyday, hanging formed an important part of Odin worship, even being regarded as a shortcut to Valhalla. The great Viking raid of 842 on Nantes in north-western France can thus be seen as the outcome of a barbarous pledge to the god. Most of the city's inhabitants were slain and hanged naked or clothed from trees. It was "an axe-age, sword-age", a violent interlude prior to the end of the world that would come at Ragnarok.

In addition to FRIGG, his wife in Asgard, Odin had many other wives, and he fathered a number of children. Among those said to be his sons were THOR, BALDER, HODR, and VALI.

Odin kept himself informed about the affairs of the nine worlds with two faithful ravens. As Vikings at sea sent out ravens in search of land, Odin's own ravens HUGINN and Muninn flew about and then "whispered into his ears every scrap of news which they saw or heard tell of". The birds' names mean "thought" and "memory" respectively. Because of his wisdom and his knowledge of events, Odin was oppressed by the approach of Ragnarok. Just as the cycle of Germanic mythology started with a cosmos awash with the blood of the original frost giant YMIR, when Odin and his brothers VILI and VE carved the world of men out of his dead body, so the final scene was to be a battlefield, where the gods were predestined to gush out their own blood. Ragnarok, the doom of the gods, began with the death of Odin's son Balder and the realization by the gods that in Loki, the god of fire, they had tolerated the growth of evil. There was nothing that Odin could do to prevent the catastrophe. His only consolation was the foreknowledge that his resurrected son Balder would be worshipped in his stead in a new age and a new land which would rise from the sea. (See also THE VALKYRIES; SORCERY AND SPELLS; RINGS OF POWER; RAGNAROK)

P

OTTAR was the human lover of *FREYJA*, the Germanic fertility goddess, and was said to be a distant descendant of the hero *SIGURD*. The warrior caught the goddess's attention through grand sacrifices. He built a stone altar and turned it into glass by the constant heat of the fire he used in preparing his bloody offering. Freyja transformed him into a boar so that she could keep him with her in *ASGARD*, the home of the gods. She even used the disguised Ottar as a mount. Ottar may have been a leader of a warrior band, a lover pleasing to Freyja who shared those fallen in battle with Odin. In the myth it is suggested that he is related to the berserkers, warriors who, "howling and foaming in frenzy, left a trail of terror and leaped like wildfire over land and sea"

OTTER, in Germanic mythology, was the son of the magician-farmer *HREIDMAR*. When the fire god *LOKI* killed him by mistake, for he had taken the shape of an otter, Hreidmar demanded compensation. The otter's flayed skin was to be covered inside and out with gold. Loki succeeded in taking as much gold as he needed from the dwarf *ANDVARI*, and insisted that he also be given a ring which

Andvari tried to conceal. Andvari cursed both the ring and the gold, saying that whoever owned them would be destroyed by them. Loki put the ring on his own finger and returned to Hreidmar with the gold. There was enough to cover the whole skin, except for one whisker; so Loki was compelled to hand over the ring as well, and the curse passed to Hreidmar.

PATOLLO was the Baltic war god, the equivalent of Germanic *ODIN*, the one-eyed god of battle, magic, inspiration and the dead. He was depicted as an old man with a long green beard and death-like pallor, wearing a turban. His sacred objects were the skulls of a man, a horse and a cow.

Patollo was the chief god of the Baltic region. He bestowed good fortune and, like Odin, he took it away whenever he had a desire to taste human blood. At some point before the advent of Christianity Patollo seems to have taken on a more pronounced role in respect of the dead. This would explain why Christian missionaries immediately identified him with the Devil.

PERKONIS see *PERKUNO*

PERKONS see *PERKUNO*

PERKUNAS see *PERKUNO*

PERKUNO (which probably meant "striker"), known as Perkunas in Lithunia, Perkons or Perkonis in Latvia, was the Baltic thunder god. He was obviously connected with the Slavic god *PERUNU*, although Perkuno was the standard European god of the storm. He was depicted as an angry-looking middle-aged man with a fiery face and a curly black beard. An order of priests is known to have maintained a perpetual fire as part of Perkuno's worship.

Baltic mythology appears to have possessed three main gods, not unlike the Germanic trio

worshipped at Uppsala in Sweden. There the war god *ODIN*, the thunder god *THOR* and the fertility god *FREYR* were revered, whereas at Romowe in Prussia, Baltic peoples gave worship to *PATOLLO*, Perkuno and *POTRIMPO*. The young, beardless god Potrimpo was the Baltic Freyr; grim Patollo was the Baltic Odin; and the Baltic Thor was Perkuno, as quick to anger as the giant-killing Germanic thunder god. A late account of the Balts even supposes a migration from Sweden in the sixth century.

Unfortunately, next to nothing of Baltic mythology has survived, apart from the names of gods and goddesses. It is of considerable interest, therefore, that Perkuno

appears in a surviving myth about *SAULE*, the sun goddess, and the moon god *MENU*. According to this tale, the moon chose not to appear in the sky with the sun because of Perkuno, who had an affair with Saule. Their love-child was the Morning Star. Whereas the sun goddess carried on as if nothing had happened and continued to show herself to all humankind during the day, Menu made himself visible only by night.

PERUN see *PERUNU*

PERUNU, known as Pyerun in Russia, Piorun in Poland and sometimes Perun, was the Slavic thunder god. He was the chief god and a creator god. At Kiev in Russia he had an important temple until the tenth century. Perunu's supremacy was ended by Vladimir, the ruler of Kiev who was later raised to the sainthood. After living the typical life of a Slavic prince, with numerous wives and mistresses, Vladimir

"tired of the desire for women" and sought a new way of living. He sent out ambassadors to witness the religious ceremonies of both the Catholic and Orthodox churches, as well as those of the Jews and

PERUNU roamed the thundery sky on his millstone, flashing shafts of lightning from his thunderbolt. In his effigy at Kiev, he appeared with a silver head and golden moustache. He was transformed into St Elijah with the arrival of Christianity,
(ILLUSTRATION BY NICK BEALE, 1995.)

Moslems. His choice fell on the Byzantine form of Christianity and thereafter the Russians and the Greeks shared the same form of Christian worship.

Prior to this conversion in 988 though, the "Rus" owed more to north-western Europe, for the establishment of the Russian state resulted from Viking trade and settlement on its great rivers. The Viking leader Oleg had captured Kiev in 882 and raised its status to "mother of Russian cities". With this Germanic influx, it is hardly surprising that there are obvious parallels between Perunu and THOR. Oleg was referred to as a "wizard". It seems quite likely that Thor provided the native Slavic thunder god with a developed mythology, since surviving details of Perunu's worship suggest that he was originally believed to be an aid to agriculture. Indeed, rain-making ceremonies are known to have involved a chaste girl, naked and decked with flowers, dancing in a magic circle. Whirling and drinking seem to have been important in his Russian worship.

PERKUNO can be seen here riding with his divine companions: on the left, young Potrimpo, crowned with fruitful wheat; next, veteran Patollo bears a skull symbolizing his affinity with war and death, while his horned turban recalls his sacred cow. Perkuno, at right, flashes his lightning.
(ILLUSTRATION BY JAMES ALEXANDER, 1995.)

PERUNU, as a fertility god, wandered over the earth, spreading summer sun, chasing away clouds and melting the snow. A god with a social sense, he bombarded the lands of the wicked with hailstorms. The oak, his sacred tree, was burned in his honour.
(ILLUSTRATION BY NICK BEALE, 1995.)

Elsewhere in Europe the Slavic peoples also revered Perunu, as place names still indicate. In Slovenia there is Perunji Ort, in Croatia Peruna Dubrava, in Bulgaria Perin Planina, and in Poland Peruny as well as Piorunow. According to Procopius, secretary to the Greek general Belisarius in the sixth century, the Slavs worshipped above all the god of lightning, and sacrificed cattle and other animals to him. In Russian folklore the memories of Perunu's great skill with the thunderbolt can doubtless be found in stories that tell of dragon-slaying and other supernatural deeds that required enormous strength.

PIORUN see *PERUNU*

POTRIMPO was the Baltic god of fertility and the equivalent of the Germanic fertility god *FREYR*, though he was also associated with rivers. He was depicted as a happy young man without a beard and crowned with ears of grain.

PYERUN see *PERUNU*

R

RAGNAROK was the doom of the Germanic gods. After a terrible winter lasting three years, a final battle would be fought between the gods and the frost giants on the *VIGRID* Plain. On the side of *ODIN* and the gods were ranged the "glorious dead" who had fallen in battle and were taken to live in *VALHALLA*; while with the fire god *LOKI* and the frost giants fought the "unworthy dead" from *HEL* (the Germanic netherworld), plus the fearsome wolf *FENRIR* and the sea monster *JORMUNGAND*. There was nothing that the chief god Odin could do to prevent this catastrophe. His only consolation was the foreknowledge that Ragnarok was not the end of the cosmos. After he had been killed by Fenrir, *THOR* had been overcome by Jormungand, and most of the other gods had died in the mutually destructive encounter with the frost giants, a new world was destined to "rise again out of the water, fair and green".

Before the battle two humans, *LIF* and Lifthrasir, had taken shelter in the sacred tree *YGGDRASIL* and they emerged after the carnage was over to repopulate the earth. Several of the gods also survived, among them Odin's sons *VIDAR* and *VALI*, and his brother *HONIR*, Thor's sons Modi and *MAGNI*, who inherited their father's hammer, and *BALDER* who came back from the dead.

Ragnarok held a great appeal for the Vikings, whose onslaught on western Europe is still the stuff of legend. Once they understood the effectiveness of the *standhogg*, the short, sharp shore-raid against the richer lands to the west and south, then, as Alcuin remarked in the eighth century, "no one is free from fear". In 793 the British offshore monastery of Lindisfarne was sacked and St Cuthbert's church was spattered with the blood of the monks. "Never before in Britain," Alcuin lamented, "has such terror appeared as this we have now

RAGNAROK (above) was foreshadowed by a chilling Fimbul winter. Sol and Mani grew pale with fear; blizzards swept down from the peaks and icebergs towered over the frozen earth. Loki broke free from his bonds and set sail with the fiery host.
(ILLUSTRATION BY JAMES ALEXANDER, 1995.)

RAGNAROK's (left) war raged on the icy Plain of Vigrid. Here, Odin wrestles with the snarling wolf, Fenrir, while Thor slays the monstrous world serpent, Jormungand, though dying from its fatal venom. At left, Loki wrestles with the bright god, Heimdall, and both gods die in the conflict. (ILLUSTRATION BY JAMES ALEXANDER, 1995.)

suffered at the hands of the heathen." But for the Vikings it was like Ragnarok, "an axe-age, a sword-age". It was a rehearsal for the "wind-age and wolf-age before the world is wrecked". Although Christianity did eventually come to the Germanic peoples of northern Europe, their preoccupation with a cosmic catastrophe did not fade altogether. The Last Judgement exercised their minds during the Middle Ages. It may well have been that behind the Nazis' resolve to fight on in World War Two lay a folk memory of Ragnarok.

RAN see *NATURE SPIRITS*

REGIN and his brother *FAFNIR* slew their father, the magician *HREIDMAR*, while under the spell of a cursed ring, Andvarinaut, which made them covet their father's gold. While Fafnir turned into a dragon in order to protect his gold, Regin settled down as a smith in the royal Danish household. There he tutored the young hero *SIGURD* and urged him to overcome Fafnir, which he did. But, equally as corrupted by the curse as his brother, Regin then plotted to murder Sigurd. However, he reckoned without the young hero's insight: Sigurd was forewarned by the birds and killed Regin first.

REIDMAR see *HREIDMAR*

RHINE MAIDENS see *NATURE SPIRITS*

RIG was the name assumed by the Germanic god *HEIMDALL* when he created the three categories of men: the slave or *thrall*; the free peasant or *karl*; and the noble or chieftain, known as *jarl*. Though usually imagined as the watchman of the gods, scanning the horizon for the final frost giant attack at Ragnarok, Heimdall was also identified with Rig, or "king". According to Rig's myth, the god once approached the lowly dwelling of an old couple,

Ai and Edda (literally "great-grand-father" and "great-grandmother"). After introducing himself as a lone wayfarer, Rig was given coarse food to satisfy his hunger and a place in the bed between them when it was time to sleep. Rig stayed three nights and gave them good advice. Nine months afterwards Edda bore a son, Thrall, who was black-haired and ugly, with rough skin, thick fingers, short nails, swollen knuckles, long heels and bent back; but he was strong. Thrall took as his wife an equally ungainly person, a drudge with crooked legs, dirty feet, sunburned arms and a big nose. Their many children included boys like Noisy, Roughneck and Horsefly, as well as girls such as Lazybones, Fatty and Beanpole. From these ill-favoured children descended the thralls, the enslaved labourers of the oppressed class. Eddar's son Thrall himself perfectly sums up the back-breaking toil of his oppressed class, weighed down with generations of hard labour.

Rig visited a second house, warm and better furnished. Inside

RIG wandered throughout the earth, visiting its people and fathering three classes of men, the thralls or serfs, karls or freemen and jarls or earls. Here, Rig sups with aged rustics in their seashore hut, gazing with pride at his first mortal child, Thrall, who was a born labourer and father of the serfs. (ILLUSTRATION BY NICK BEALE, 1995.)

he encountered an industrious couple, Afi and Amma (literally "grandfather" and "grandmother"). The well-dressed pair were spinning and weaving: Afi prepared a loom, Amma spun a thread. Once again Rig shared their table and bed, gave good advice and departed after three nights. Nine months afterwards Amma bore a son, Karl, who was red and fresh and bright-eyed. Karl took to wife Snor (meaning "daughter-in-law") and their children included boys named Strongbeard, Husbandman and Smith, and girls called Prettyface, Maiden and Capable. Together they ran farms and were free.

A third dwelling Rig stayed at was a splendid hall belonging to Fadir and Modir ("father" and "mother"). While Fadir attended to his bow and arrows, Modir saw to her own looks and clothes. After a large meal, accompanied by fine conversation and drink, Rig slept between his well-off hosts. He stayed three nights and gave good advice. Nine months afterwards Modir bore a son, Jarl, who was fair-haired and handsome, with a bright cheek and an eye as piercing as a serpent's. When he grew to manhood, Jarl could use bow, spear, sword and shield; he could ride and swim and hunt expertly. One day Rig returned and greeted Jarl as his special son, imparting wisdom and telling him how to claim his lands. In obedience to the

REGIN reforges the shards of Sigurd's wondrous sword, Gram. Once mended, the sword was so strong and sharp that it split the iron anvil in two. With it, Sigurd slew Regin's brother, Fafnir, who had turned himself into a dragon so that he could guard his gold. (WOOD CARVING, 12TH CENTURY.)

RIG next visited a thrifty farmhouse where he was hospitably entertained by Amma and Afi. Rig stayed for three days and fathered a fine sturdy, blue-eyed boy, named Karl, who grew up to be a natural farmer. Here, Karl and his wife, Snor, can be seen working their fruitful land. (ILLUSTRATION BY NICK BEALE, 1995.)

god, Jarl rode through the world, fighting and slaying, seizing booty and distributing treasure to his free followers. At last he married Erna ("lively"), a fair and wise noblewoman, and she bore him twelve sons. One of these learned magic so well that he could prevent forest fires, control storms and cure the sick. It was said that he excelled even Rig in understanding and almost became a god. The implication is that in his person he combined the roles of priest and king.

The myth of Rig sheds light on the structure of Viking society. In contrast with the Celts, the other main tribal people of pre-Christian Europe, the Germanic tribes of Scandinavia and northern Europe had already lost a priestly class by the time we encounter their mythology. As Julius Caesar noted, the ancient Germans had no equivalent of the druids and cared little for ritual. They found religious significance in the depths of forests. But the Romans, and later the Vikings' victims, were in no doubt about the Germanic love of warfare and the role of the armed retainer, the sturdy free peasant, in battle.

SORCERY AND SPELLS

SORCERY AMONG THE NORSEMEN was a unique and precious art practised essentially by Odin and the Vanir deities of nature, but also by dwarfs and some privileged mortals, usually women. Although distinguished heroes, such as Sigurd, were blessed with magical weapons, they usually lacked any magical powers. Odin, the arch-sorcerer, developed his skills over a lifetime of search and sacrifice, much like a mortal shaman. Ever thirsty for wisdom and power, he wandered the nine worlds as a vagrant, clad in a blue mantle and slouch hat, gathering and garnering every snippet of information he could find. After hanging himself on the World Tree, he learnt the secrets of the dead and restored himself to life. By contrast, the heroes of Finnish myth were often gifted from birth with astounding magical powers and arcane wisdom. The wise wizard, Vainamoinen, was a born sage and sorcerer, while debonair Leminkainen was bathed as a baby to imbue him with wisdom and sorcery. Equipped with a repertoire of sacred songs, the Finns penetrated to the roots of life. Finnish sorcerers were so famous that in medieval times Norwegian kings forbade people to sail to Finnmark for the purpose of consulting magicians.

KULLERVO *curses Ilmarinen's wicked wife who had taunted him beyond endurance, giving him a dry loaf for his lunch, stuffed with a rock which shattered his family knife. In response, he turned her gentle cows into bears which devoured her at the milking. Kullervo, a tortured soul, unloved from birth, responded to the world's sleights with distorted malice. Gifted with powerful sorcery, he punished his enemies beyond their crime.* (THE CURSE OF KULLERVO BY A GALLEN-KALLELA, CANVAS, C. 1850.)

VAINAMOINEN (above) fends off the griffin perched on his ship. The monster was the sorceress, Louhi, who had turned herself into a metallic bird. She was after the talisman, the Sampo. Just as she reared to strike the final blow, Vainamoinen raised his rudder and crushed her talons. The Sampo was broken and scattered, but Vainamoinen gathered some fragments and partly restored its power. (DEFENCE OF THE SAMPO BY A GALLEN-KALLELA, CANVAS, 1852.)

KULLERVO (above), doomed from birth, set out on his last journey, piping loudly on his cow horn, his mother's Blackie dog running behind. En route he passed a blasted stretch of green where he had unwittingly despoiled his long-lost sister. Here the meadow grasses bemoaned the maiden's terrible fate. Feeling the crushing weight of guilt and a lifetime of bitterness, Kullervo eventually threw himself on his sword. Although a powerful sorcerer, Kullervo was denied love throughout his life and never learnt the way of things. (KULLERVO BY A GALLEN-KALLELA, CANVAS, C. 1850.)

FREYJA (right) was renowned for her magical crafts, along with the other Vanir deities of fertility and nature. She was the first to teach the warrior Aesir the practice of seior or magic. Seior was useful but could be dangerous, giving its practitioners foreknowledge and power over life and death, love and intelligence. Odin quickly learnt all that Freyja could teach him and, ever thirsty for knowledge, surpassed the Vanir in magic arts. In later myth, Freyja was identified with Idun, goddess of Spring who guarded the magic apples of youth, seen here. (ILLUSTRATION BY ARTHUR RACKHAM, C. 1910.)

A RING OF FIRE (far left) encircled the Valkyrie, Brynhild, protecting her in an enchanted sleep from all but the bravest. Only Sigurd dared the fiery circle of flames to win the sleeping beauty. His fearless spirit carried him through, mysteriously unharmed, as predicted by the birds whose song he understood. (ILLUSTRATION BY H THEAKER, C. 1920.)

GRIMHILD (left), Queen of the Niebelungs, was famed and feared for her magic. With her spells and potions, she could erase a person's memory and control his will. When she offered unsuspecting Sigurd her magic mead, he forgot his love for Brynhild and instead fell in love with Grimhild's daughter, Gudrun. (ILLUSTRATION BY ARTHUR RACKHAM, C. 1910.)

S

RIND (above), *a cool Nordic princess, became ill with a mystery malady and was nursed back to health by Odin in disguise. The old nurse, Vecha, restored Rind to health, first by bathing her in a hot bath. The warm water thawed her frozen heart and symbolized the melting of the frozen rind of earth.* (ILLUSTRATION BY NICK BEALE, 1995.)

THE RUSALKI (right) *dwelt in rivers and lakes. The southern sprites were pearly beauties who lured travellers with their sweet song. During Rusalki Week, which was at the start of summer, they emerged from the rivers to dwell and dance in the forests, enriching the grass in their wake.* (ILLUSTRATION BY ALAN LEE, 1984.)

RIND, in Germanic mythology, was the daughter of King *BILLING* and the mistress of *ODIN*, who pursued her in various disguises. Their love led to the birth of *VALI*, the child who was to avenge the death of *BALDER*. In one version, Odin was deposed as king of the gods for forcing Rind to submit simply in order that he might father a son.

ROSKVA was a farmer's daughter who became a servant of the god *THOR*. When Thor stopped at her father's house and asked for food and shelter they were too poor to provide meat, so Thor offered his own goats on the condition that no bones were broken. But Roskva's brother *THIALFI* broke one of the thigh bones and when Thor came to resurrect the goats one of them had a limp. The enraged god was only pacified by the promised service of Roskva and Thialfi, who travelled with him thereafter.

THE RUSALKI were water nymphs and can be found in both Slavonic and Russian mythology. They were thought to be the spirits of drowned girls. During the winter months, they lived in the great rivers of eastern Europe, taking on different forms in different regions. For instance, in the Rivers Dnieper and Danube, in south-eastern Europe, they were commonly pictured as beautiful, siren-like creatures who would attempt to lure unsuspecting passers-by into the water with their magical song. In the northern regions, in contrast, the water nymphs were considered to be malevolent, unkempt and unattractive creatures, who would grab travellers from the river banks and drag them down into the river and drown them. During the summer, when the rivers were warmed by the sun, the Rusalki came out of the water on to the land and lived in the cool of the forests.

SAMPO see *TREASURES AND TALISMANS*

SAULE was the Baltic sun goddess and, according to one tradition, the mistress of the thunder god *PERKUNO*. She was worshipped by Lithuanians, Prussians and Letts before they were converted to Christianity. Her worship took the form of looking after a harmless green snake. Every house kept one: under the bed, in a corner, even under the table. Apart from ensuring a household's wealth and fertility, the kindness shown to the snake was regarded as a guarantee of Saule's generosity. To kill a snake was an act of sacrilege. The sight of a dead one was believed to bring tears to the eyes of the sun goddess. Even after the conversion of the Lithuanians to Christianity in the fifteenth century – they were the last people to be Christianized on the continent – the peasants continued to revere green snakes. It was long held that seeing one in the countryside meant that either a marriage or birth would follow.

Saule was imagined as pouring light from a jug. The golden liquid which she generously gave to the world was the basis of life itself, the warmth so necessary after the cold north-eastern European winter. Another fragment of myth about Saule concerns the Baltic equivalent of the Greek Dioscuri, who were the divine twins Castor and Polydeuces. The unnamed Baltic twins are said to have rescued Saule from the sea and built a barn in which the goddess could rest.

SIEGFRIED see *SIGURD*

SIEGMUND see *TRAGIC LOVERS*

SIF was the wife of *THOR*, the Germanic thunder god, and the mother, by a previous marriage, of Uu, god of archery and skiing. She is the subject of a strange myth in which the trickster *LOKI*, the god of fire, one night cut off her beautiful golden hair, probably a representation of ripe corn and therefore fertility. Next morning Thor was beside himself with rage at Sif's distress. When Loki protested that it was only a joke, Thor demanded to know what he was going to do about it, and the fire god said he would get the dwarfs to weave a wig as a replacement.

So Loki asked the sons of Ivaldi to make a wig from spun gold. The completed piece of work was quite remarkable, for it was so light that a breath of air was enough to ruffle its skeins and so real that it grew on her head by magic. Thinking to get the gods even more into their debt, the sons of Ivaldi used the remaining heat in their furnace to construct a collapsible ship named *Skidbladnir* for the fertility god *FREYR* and a magic spear called *GUNGNIR* for *ODIN*. On his way back to *ASGARD*, the stronghold of the gods, crossing the underground

SAULE (above), the Baltic sun goddess, poured golden light from her heavenly height through the summery clouds down to the earth below. The snake on her crown symbolizes her fertility and abundance. The Morning Star, her child, flashes above her. (ILLUSTRATION BY JAMES ALEXANDER, 1995.)

SIF (above right) was famous for her gold, flowing hair, symbolizing ripe harvest corn. When Loki cut off her locks her misery represented the winter season when the cornfields are reduced to stubble. Here, Loki lurks menacingly behind the dreaming beauty. (ILLUSTRATION BY NICK BEALE, 1995.)

SIGNY (right) Queen of Gotaland, rushes down the glacial fjord to greet her kinsmen. She warns them of an ambush planned by her vengeful husband, Siggeir, a sore loser, who bitterly resented her brother Sigmund's victory in a magical sword contest. (ILLUSTRATION BY JAMES ALEXANDER, 1995.)

caverns where the dwarfs lived, Loki also met the dwarf brothers Brokk and Eiti. They were so jealous of the workmanship that had gone into the wig, the boat and the spear that Loki persuaded them to make something better; he even staked his own head on their inability to do so. As a result, the dwarf brothers fashioned the magic hammer known as *MJOLLNIR*, the scourge of the frost giants.

The gods were delighted with the treasures Loki and Brokk had brought back. However, Brokk demanded Loki's head. The gods would not agree, but they had no objection to Brokk sewing up Loki's lips with a thong when Thor dragged the god back home after

he tried to flee, which caused Loki to plan a revenge against Thor. (See also *TREASURES AND TALISMANS*)

SIGMUND see NORSE HEROES

SIGNY, in Germanic mythology, was the unfortunate daughter of *VOLSUNG*, supposedly a descendant of *ODIN*. Married against her will to the Gothic king Siggeir, she tried to warn her father and her ten

brothers about Siggeir's plot against them, but they were ambushed in a forest and bound to a fallen tree. Each night a wolf devoured one of them in turn, until only her youngest brother Sigmund was left alive. Signy got a slave to smear Sigmund's face with honey so that the wolf would lick him instead of biting him. Sigmund was thus able to catch the wolf's tongue in his teeth and overcome the beast.

Signy helped Sigmund to plot revenge. She even slept with him in disguise and bore a son named Sinfiotli. When Sinfiotli grew up she placed him in Sigmund's care, but they were both captured by Siggeir. A magic sword freed them and killed Siggeir and his sons. Signy chose to die herself in the burning Gothic palace, but not before she had told Sigmund the truth about Sinfiotli's parentage.

SIGRYN see SIGYN

SIGUNN see SIGYN

SIGURD, or Siegfried as he was known in German, was a northern Germanic hero similar to the Celtic King Arthur. He was the foster-son of *REGIN*, the smith at the court of King Hjalprek in Jutland, who sent him to recover a fabulous hoard of gold. Regin's father *HREIDMAR* had first acquired this treasure, which once belonged to the dwarf *ANDVARI*. To get their hands on the gold Regin and his brother *FAFNIR* had then killed Hreidmar, but Fafnir wanted the treasure for himself and turned into a dragon to guard it. By cunningly stabbing the monster from underneath, Sigurd succeeded in slaying Fafnir, thus apparently gaining both dwarfish wealth and wisdom, since Fafnir was said to have understood the language of birds. When he realized that Regin intended to kill him for the gold, Sigurd slew him before carrying it away himself. (See also *NORSE HEROES*; *TRAGIC LOVERS*; *RINGS OF POWER*)

SIGYN, also known as Sigunn or Sigryn, in Germanic mythology, was the faithful wife of the fire god *LOKI* and mother of his sons Narvi and *VALI*. Once the gods realized that in Loki they had allowed the growth of evil in their midst, they

SIGURD (above) watches with fascination as Regin forges the broken shards of his father's wondrous sword, a gift from Odin. The conquering sword would help Sigurd in his destined mission to slay the dragon, Fafnir, guardian of a fabulous but ill-fated treasure. (SIEGFRIED IN THE FORGE OF REGIN BY W VON HANSCHILD, FRESCO, 1880.)

SIGURD (right) confronts the fire-breathing dragon, Fafnir, and slays him, winning fame and a fateful fortune. On the advice of his mentor, Regin, he roasted the creature's heart, licking some spilt blood from which he learnt the speech of birds. (SIEGFRIED AND FAFNIR BY H. HENRICH, CANVAS, 1906.)

SIGURD (above) exults in his wondrous new weapon, anticipating victory over his frightful foe, Fafnir. Equipped with the sharpest blade and nerves of iron, the eager hero set off excitedly on his first quest. This striking portrayal highlights the youthful idealism of the zealous Nordic hero. (ILLUSTRATION BY ARTHUR RACKHAM, C. 1900.)

SIGYN (above), the devoted wife of Loki, stood by him even after he had been banished to an icy prison. There she lessened his pain by catching the fiery venom dribbled by a serpent tied above his face. When she went to empty the bowl, he writhed in agony, shaking the earth. (LOKI AND SIGYN BY M E WINGE, CANVAS, C. 1890.)

SKIRNIR (above) gallops through a fiery ring guarding the icy home of Gerda, a frost giantess. On a mission to win Gerda for his gentle master, Freyr, Skirnir bears gifts of life-giving apples, a multiplying ring, Draupnir, and a glowing portrait of Freyr, captured in his drinking horn. (ILLUSTRATION BY GLENN STEWARD, 1995.)

bound him in a cave. First they took hold of three slabs of rock, stood them on end and bored a hole through each of them. Then the entrails of Loki's son Narvi were employed as a rope which bound the fire god to the stones. When the gods had tied the last knot, the entrails became as hard as iron. To ensure Loki's discomfort the frost giantess SKADI, NJORD's wife, fastened a snake to a stalactite above the god's head and there he was to remain until RAGNAROK.

Despite all that her husband had done, Sigyn remained true to him and did what she could to lessen his suffering by catching the venom dripping from the snake in a wooden bowl. However, whenever she went away to empty its poisonous contents, the venom fell on Loki's head and caused him to twitch violently. According to the Vikings, it was these compulsive movements that accounted for earthquakes.

SKADE see SKADI

SKADI, a cool and independent huntress, roamed the mountains on her snow shoes. A spirit of winter, she was far happier on her icy slopes than in her husband's sunlit coves. A deity of hunters and mountain climbers, she guided their sleighs over the snow. (ILLUSTRATION BY JAMES ALEXANDER, 1995.)

SKADI, or Skade (which means "destruction"), was a figure in northern Germanic mythology. She was the wife of the sea god NJORD and daughter of the frost giant THIASSI. When the gods of ASGARD killed her father for stealing IDUN's apples, Skadi armed herself and went to the gods' stronghold to seek compensation. Refusing an offer of gold, she demanded a husband and a bellyful of laughter. This was agreed, provided that Skadi chose her husband by his feet only. Thinking that the most shapely feet must surely belong to handsome BALDER, ODIN's son, Skadi made her choice only to discover that she had picked Njord. The merriment was provided by LOKI, who tied his testicles to a goat. As the couple were unable to stand the conditions in each other's homes, Njord and Skadi decided that it was best to live apart. Her relationship with the gods continued, however, and it was she who placed the venomous snake above Loki's head when the gods eventually imprisoned the troublesome god in a cave.

SKIRNIR ("Shining") was a servant of FREYR, the Germanic god of fertility. When Freyr wished to marry the frost giantess GERDA, he promised Skirnir his horse and his sword and sent him to JOTUNHEIM, the land of the frost giants. Skirnir had some difficulty in persuading Gerda to agree to the match, however. Eleven apples of youth, the magic fruit that kept the gods young, were no temptation to her. Nor was one of Odin's arm-rings. Gerda showed no fear when Skirnir threatened to behead her, but she began to panic the moment he started to recite a powerful spell. It promised to deny her any joy or passion, for the beautiful frost giantess was to be transformed into a loveless outcast, a companion of the "unworthy dead". As a result of this threatened fate, Gerda at last consented to meet Freyr and so Skirnir received his promised rewards. On another occasion, Skirnir acted in his role as messenger by going to the dwarfs on Odin's behalf to order a magical fetter so that Odin could restrain the terrible wolf FENRIR.

SKOLL, in Germanic mythology, was a wolf that pursued the sun in her flight across the sky. At *RAGNAROK*, the doom of the gods, Skoll was destined to seize the sun between his jaws and swallow her. Just before this happened, though, the sun would give birth to a daughter as beautiful as herself and this new sun would warm and illuminate the new earth risen from the sea, "fresh and green", following the catastrophe. Another wolf, named Hati, chased after the moon. Both creatures were said to be the sons of a giantess living in Iron Wood.

Ravenous dogs often threatened to eat the heavenly bodies in the myths of northern parts of both Europe and Asia. Chinese families today still bang cooking utensils to frighten "the dog of heaven" during a lunar eclipse.

SKOLL (below), a fierce wolf, symbolizing Repulsion, chased the sun across the sky, from dawn to dusk. Skoll's sole aim in life was to overtake and devour the heavenly orb, plunging the world into primordial darkness. (ILLUSTRATION BY GLENN STEWARD, 1995.)

SKRYMIR ("Vast") was an extra large frost giant in Germanic mythology. So huge was he that on a journey through the land of giants *THOR* and *LOKI*, along with their servants *THIALFI* and *ROSKVA*, inadvertently slept in the thumb of Skrymir's empty glove, thinking it was a hall. When Thor later tried to hammer in the skull of the sleeping Skrymir, the frost giant awoke in the belief that either a leaf or an acorn had dropped on his brow. Afterwards it dawned on Thor and his companions that Skrymir was a gigantic illusion, a magic creation sent out by the frost giants in order to prevent them from reaching *UTGARD*, the giants' citadel.

SLEIPNIR ("Glider"), was the eight-legged horse ridden by *ODIN*, the chief of the Germanic gods. This fabulous creature was the offspring of an unusual union between Svadilfari, a stallion of great strength, and *LOKI*, the shape-changer, who had disguised himself as a mare. Sleipnir could travel over sea and through the air, and was swift enough to beat any other horse in a race. At *RAGNAROK*, Sleipnir was the horse that carried Odin into battle.

SOL see *NATURE SPIRITS*

SURT ("Black"), in Germanic mythology, was a fire giant with a flaming blade who would set the cosmos alight at *RAGNAROK*. He was identified with the fire god *LOKI*. At Ragnarok Surt was to rise from Muspell, the land of flame, and fling fire in every direction. The nine worlds were to become raging furnaces as gods, frost giants, the

SLEIPNIR (above), the fabulous eight-hoofed (or some say, eight-legged) steed of Odin, certainly deserved his name "Glider" for he slipped through cloud, sea or earth with equal ease. Sleipnir's hooves rumbled in the storm clouds when Odin travelled across the sky as god of the winds. (ILLUSTRATION BY GLENN STEWARD, 1995.)

SVANTOVIT (right), the four-headed war god of the Slavs, guarded the world on four sides. His stone effigy at Rugen was worshipped before battle. As a deity of fertility, plenty and destiny, he bore a horn of plenty and rode a horse of divination. A white horse was kept in the temple for ritual divination. (ILLUSTRATION BY NICK BEALE, 1995.)

SURT (below), a fierce fire giant, rose from the furnace of Muspell at Ragnarok to lead his fiery hordes against the divine host. With his flaming sword, he set the nine worlds ablaze, burning them to blackened cinders which sank beneath the boiling ocean only to rise again fresh, green and new. (ILLUSTRATION BY JAMES ALEXANDER, 1995.)

dead, the living, monsters, dwarfs, elves and animals were all to be reduced to ashes. Then the earth would sink into the sea, before rising again, fresh and green. It may be that the view of the end of the world as an immense conflagration was influenced by the volcanic nature of Iceland, from where many of the written myths originated. In 1963–7, a new island, formed by a volcanic eruption off the coast of Iceland, was named Surtsey after the god Surt.

SVANTEVIT see *SVANTOVIT*

SVANTOVIT, also known as Svantevit, was the war god of the Slavic peoples of central Europe. His temple at Arcona on the Baltic island of Rugen was destroyed by King Valdemar of Denmark and his Christian adviser Absalon in 1169.

The building contained a four-headed statue of Svantovit that was nearly thirty feet in height. Multiple heads were indeed a feature of the Slavic pantheon. It is thought that Svantovit may also have been worshipped as a supreme deity and seen as a father to other gods.

Prior to the Danish destruction of the temple in the Christian era, the worshippers of Svantovit at Arcona believed that the god would mount a sacred white horse and ride out at nights against those who denied his divinity. In the morning the horse was often discovered to be covered in sweat. Omens for success in war were read from the behaviour of the sacred horse as well. Human sacrifices, which were a widespread custom throughout the Germanic and Slavic peoples, were made to Svantovit before any great undertakings, .

SVARAZIC, sometimes Svarozic or Svarogich (which probably meant "hot" or "torrid" – a meaning that can still be found today in the Romanian language), was the Slavic fire god, especially of the fire that was used to dry grain. He was the son of Svaroz, or Svarog (who was identified with the Greek smith god Hephaistos) and the brother of *DAZHBOG*. The fire god was depicted wearing a helmet and carrying a sword, and on his breast was a black bison's head. Human sacrifices were made to Svarazic, including, after his capture in 1066, the German bishop of Mecklenburg. In some traditions, Svarazic was identified with the flame of lightning.

SVAROGICH see *SVARAZIC*

SVAROZIC see *SVARAZIC*

TRAGIC LOVERS

TIMELESS TALES OF TRAGIC LOVE are common everywhere, yet rarely so stark and bleak as in Norse mythology. Sometimes a curse lies at the root of the trouble, as in the tale of Sigurd and Brynhild, where a cursed ring wrecks the lives of several pairs of doomed lovers. Sometimes the trials of love symbolize the battles of nature. Sigurd, for instance, might be seen as a sun lord who, armed with a sunbeam, dispels darkness; while his lover, Brynhild, symbolizes the dawn-maiden whose path he crosses only at the start and close of his shining career. In other tales, obstacles simply serve to test the lovers' honour and courage, as when Frithiof faithfully guards his sleeping rival, Sigurd Ring. In their love affairs, the gods seem luckier than mortals, though friction is rife, if short-lived, as when Odur flees Freyja or Skadi lives apart from Njord. Such conflict might symbolize seasonal changes: Njord's sunny love can only hold wintry Skadi for three months of the year. By contrast, in the heart-warming tale of the summer god, Freyr, he wins his frosty bride by sheer warmth of love which melts her icy heart.

SIEGMUND and Sieglinde (left), were siblings who grew up apart, both enduring tragic fates, before meeting by chance and falling in love. Here, the lovers exchange secret glances while in the company of Sieglinde's suspicious husband, Hunding, who plans to slay Siegmund in a duel. When Siegmund wins, he and Sieglinde enjoy brief love before dying, one on the battlefield, the other in childbirth. The child of their sad union is the great hero, Sigurd. (*ILLUSTRATION BY F LEEKE, C. 1895.*)

INGEBORG (above), in the sanctuary of Balder's temple, stops spinning and pines for her lover, Frithiof. Cloistered by her watchful brothers, she was denied contact with Frithiof, who was considered beneath her royal status. Yet when Frithiof broke the sanctity of the temple to rescue Ingeborg, she refused to flee with him, believing herself honour bound to obey the wishes of her royal brothers. (*INGEBORG'S LAMENT BY F N JENSEN, CANVAS, C. 1830.*)

FREYR (left), a gentle summer god, caught a glimpse of the radiant frost giantess, Gerda, from afar and at once fell in love, but doubted his chances until his decisive servant, Skirnir, set off to woo the girl for his master. Gerda remained unmoved until she was forced by threat of magic to at least consent to a meeting with Freyr. Once in the company of the fiery god, Gerda's icy heart thawed. Freyr appears here as a dreamy summer god, bearing his wheat, with his boar at his feet, emblems of fruitful harvest. (FREYR BY E BURNE-JONES JONES, CANVAS, C. 1870.)

KREIMHILD (right) wakes from a nightmare in which she dreamt that a lovely white falcon was struck in flight by two black eagles. Her mother interprets the dream to mean that Kreimhild will eventually fall in love with a peerless prince – who is symbolized by the white bird – and that he will be killed by two murderers – the black eagles. Indeed, some years later the dream came true as Kreimhild fell in love with the great hero Sigurd, later slain by her two brothers, Gunner and Hogni, who were acting under the influence of a curse. Here, Kreimhild is depicted telling her mother about her dream, while below a bard, a poet and a Christian pontiff ponder the meaning of the Teutonic epic, the Niebelungenlied. (THE LEGEND OF SIEGFRIED BY F PILOTY, WOOD, C. 1890.)

FRITHIOF and Ingeborg (left) are at last united in Balder's temple. The childhood sweethearts had been thwarted by Ingeborg's hostile brothers. While Ingeborg was forced into a marriage with an old chieftain, Sigurd Ring, Frithiof roamed the high seas in misery. When his undying love drove him home, he waited honourably until the old king died before at last winning his bride. (FRITHIOF AND INGEBORG BY J A MALMSTROM, CANVAS, C. 1840.)

BRYNHILD and Sigurd (above) find peace together at last after a romance wrecked by a web of intrigue and vengeance. After pledging his love to Brynhild, Sigurd was bewitched into marrying Gudrun. Brynhild, in her turn, was unwittingly tricked by Sigurd into marrying Gunner. When Brynhild discovered Sigurd's apparent betrayal, she cried out for vengeance. Sigurd was slain and Brynhild, overcome by grief, killed herself to be laid to rest beside him. (THE FUNERAL PYRE BY C BUTLER, CANVAS, 1909.)

T

TANNGNOST (meaning "Tooth-gnasher"), in Germanic mythology, was the name of one of the two billy goats which pulled *THOR*'s chariot. The other was named Tanngrisnir ("Tooth-grinder"). The rumble of the chariot was heard by people on earth as the sound of thunder. Like the magic boar of *VALHALLA*, which could be eaten one day and reappear alive the next, Thor's goats provided an endless supply of meat as long as, after cooking, all their bones remained intact. Thor would then wave his magic hammer over the skin and bones and the goats came alive.

TAPIO was the Finnish forest god, who, along with his wife Meilikki and his son Nyyrikki, was believed to ensure that woodland game remained in plentiful supply. He had a dangerous side to his nature, however, as he enjoyed tickling or smothering people to death. His daughter Tuulikki was a spirit of the wind. Tapio is often portrayed as wearing a cloak of moss and a bonnet of fire.

THIALFI and his sister *ROSKVA* were the children of a farmer and servants of the Germanic thunder god *THOR*. When Thor and *LOKI* were travelling through Midgard they stopped at the farmhouse and Thor provided goats for supper on condition that all the bones be kept intact. Because Thialfi had not had a satisfying meal for a long time, he ignored this instruction and split a thigh bone to get at the marrow. Next morning, when Thor used his magic hammer to restore the goats to life, the thunder god noticed

that one animal was lame. He was so enraged that he threatened destruction of the farm and demanded compensation. He was placated only when Thialfi and Roskva were given to him as his servants. Although Thialfi lost a running contest to *HUGI* during Thor's visit to the frost giant stronghold of *UTGARD*, his master was outwitted by magic in several challenges too. In another myth Thialfi deserved Thor's gratitude when he toppled the enormous clay giant Mist Calf, which had caused Thor to panic with fear. He also fetched aid for the wounded thunder god after his duel with *HRUNGNIR*, the strongest of the frost giants.

TANNGNOST and Tanngrisnir (left) were a pair of goats who pulled Thor's chariot across the sky, creating the clatter and rumble of storm clouds. Thor alone among the gods never rode, but either strode or drove his goat-drawn chariot. (THOR AND THE GIANTS BY M E WINGE, CANVAS, C. 1890.)

TAPIO (above), a green god of the Finnish forests, dwelt in the depths of the greenwood, clad in moss, and growing a fir-like beard. Along with other sylvan deities, he was lord not just of forest plants, but also of forest beasts and the herds of woodland cattle. (ILLUSTRATION BY JAMES ALEXANDER, 1995.)

THIASSI, or Thiazi, in Germanic mythology, was a frost giant and the father of *SKADI* who stole from the goddess *IDUN* the apples of youth. It was really *LOKI*'s fault that this event occurred. Disguised as an eagle, the giant grabbed hold of the god and, to secure his own release from Thiassi, Loki promised to deliver the goddess and her magic apples into the frost giant's hands. The effect upon the gods was immediate. Without Idun's apples to eat each day, they grew anxious and old. In this crisis Odin alone had the determination to rally enough strength to plan a recovery. The gods captured the trickster Loki, and made him fly as

THIAZI see THIASSI

THOKK was the callous frost giantess of Germanic myth. After the popular god BALDER's unfortunate death, HEL, the queen of the "unworthy dead", said that she would allow him back to the land of the living on the condition that "everything in the nine worlds, dead and alive, weeps for him". Messengers were therefore sent out to ensure that everything mourned and were satisfied that they had achieved their aim. On their way back to ASGARD, however, they found Thokk in a cave, and when they explained their mission the giantess replied that she had no use for Balder and added, "Let Hel keep what she holds." Some versions of the myth maintain that Thokk was none other than LOKI.

THIASSI (left), a frost giant, disguised as an eagle, pestered Odin, Honir and Loki on a trip to Midgard. At one point Thiassi swooped down and scooped up the gods' dinner pot. Enraged, Loki lunged at the eagle with his staff but became stuck fast to the bird. (ILLUSTRATION BY PETER HURD, 1882.)

THOKK, alone among all the creatures in the nine worlds, refused to shed a single tear for Balder, so destroying his one chance of escape from Hel. Around bitter Thokk all creation weeps – the leaves, stones and snow itself – mourning the loss of the much-loved Balder. (ILLUSTRATION BY NICK BEALE, 1995.)

a falcon to Thiassi's hall in order to bring back Idun and her apples. This Loki was able to accomplish, but the frost giant almost thwarted the plan by turning himself yet again into an eagle and flying after the god. He very nearly caught up with Loki, but as Thiassi flew over ASGARD his wings were set alight by fires that the gods had placed on top of the stronghold's high walls. The giant could no longer fly and so fell to the ground, burned to death by the flames.

Eventually, Thiassi's daughter Skadi came to Asgard to seek compensation for her father's death. When her demands had been satisfied, Odin took Thiassi's eyes from his cloak and threw them into the sky as stars. "Thiassi will look down on all of us," he said, "for as long as the world lasts."

THOR was the Germanic thunder god. He was the son of ODIN, the chief god, and Fjorgyn, the goddess of earth. When the Anglo-Saxons eventually adopted the Roman calendar, they named the fifth day Thursday after Thor, for this was the day belonging to Jupiter, the Roman sky god and peer of the hot-tempered, red-headed Thor, along with the Greek Zeus and the Hindu Indra. His name means "thunder" and his magic hammer, MJOLLNIR, may once have meant "lightning". Among Icelanders and Norwegians family names like Thorsten recall the name of the god, for these farmers had little sympathy with the footloose Vikings who worshipped Odin, the father of the slain. The Icelandic colonists, who had fled southern Norway to escape the aggression of Danish and Swedish rulers, preferred honest Thor, the powerful but straightforward opponent of the frost giants.

Yet Thor, the bitter enemy of the frost giants, was in many aspects not unlike a giant himself. He was exceptionally strong, very

THOR, in his most popular guise as champion of the gods, was a tireless warrior and giant-slayer. With his red-hot hammer and belt of strength, which doubled his power, he was a formidable foe. Here, the thunder god swings his fiery missile.
(ILLUSTRATION BY ARTHUR RACKHAM, C. 1900.)

large – his frequent companion LOKI, the fire god, usually attached himself to Thor's belt – energetic and had an enormous appetite, which allowed him to eat a whole ox at one sitting. And, of course, there was his relish for a contest, a trial of strength. Two goats drew Thor's great chariot across the sky: their names were Tooth-grinder and Tooth-gnasher. His magic weapons were a hammer, really a thunderbolt; iron gauntlets, which he used to handle the red-hot hammer shaft; and a belt that increased his strength. MJOLLNIR, the hammer, was the handiwork of two dwarfs, the sons of Ivaldi. It had a huge head and a short handle and always hit its target.

Thor was the mightiest of the Germanic gods and their staunch protector against the frost giants. At RAGNAROK, the doom of the gods,

he was destined to be killed by the poisonous venom of the sea serpent JORMUNGAND, although not before Thor had killed the monster. Before he was slain by this terrible son of Loki, however, Loki and he had many adventures together.

These adventures were often dangerous for Thor, especially when Loki led the thunder god into danger as a price for his own freedom. Such was the case with their visit to the hall of the frost giant GEIRROD. Having been captured by Geirrod when Loki was in the shape of a hawk, he could avoid death only by making a promise to deliver an unarmed Thor into the frost giant's hands. Because Thor enjoyed Loki's company and was so trusting, he let the fire god lead him to Geirrod's hall without the protection of his hammer, gloves and belt. But on the

edge of JOTUNHEIM, the land of the frost giants, Thor and Loki spent the night with GRID, a friendly giantess. Grid warned Thor about Geirrod's hatred of the gods. She told him that he would be especially pleased to avenge the death of HRUNGNIR, the strongest of the frost giants whom Thor had killed in a duel. The thunder god still had a piece of this dead frost giant's throwing stone stuck in his head to prove it, so Thor was most grateful at Grid's loan of her own belt of strength, iron gloves and unbreakable staff.

Crossing a torrent of water and blood near the frost giant's hall proved difficult, until Thor blocked the source of the blood with a well-aimed stone. It struck GJALP, Geirrod's daughter, whose menstrual outpouring had swollen the river. Even then, the two gods were swept away, as Thor lost his footing and Loki clung desperately to the belt of Grid that the thunder god was wearing. Happily, Thor succeeded in grabbing a mountain ash overhanging the flood and scrambled ashore on the opposite bank.

Soon Thor and Loki arrived at Geirrod's hall, where servants grudgingly received them. The owner was nowhere to be seen, so Thor sat down in a chair to await his return. Snatching a nap, he was surprised when he dreamed he was floating in the air. Thor opened his eyes and saw that his head was about to be rammed against the ceiling. Quick as a flash, he used Grid's staff to push against the ceiling, with the result that the chair came down hard enough to crush Gjalp and Greip to death. These two daughters of Geirrod had been

of such enormous size that Thor would be struck by terror on seeing him. Named MIST CALF, the clay giant was animated by the heart of a mare and, slow moving though he was, clouds gathered round his towering head. On the day of the duel Thor wet himself at the sight of Mist Calf, although his charioteer had the good sense to topple the clay giant by attacking his legs with an axe. Mist Calf's fall shook Jotunheim, the land of the frost giants. In the fight with Hrungnir it was Thor who came off best, although the thunder god was left

THOR'S (left) hammer was a symbol of creative and destructive power and a source of fertility, renewal and good fortune. As Christianity swept north, the sign of the cross often fused with the sign of the hammer, as in this charm, containing a cross within a hammer. (SILVER, 10TH CENT.)

pinned to the ground by one of the dead frost giant's legs and with a piece of whetstone lodged in his head. None of the gods could release Thor and it was fortunate that his own three-year-old frost giant son MAGNI turned up after the fight. The son of the frost giantess Jarnsaxa, a mistress of Thor, Magni also told his flattened father how he could have dealt with Hrungnir with his bare fists. Thor was delighted to see Magni's strength and gave him the dead frost giant's steed Golden Mane as a reward, much to Odin's

THOR (below), the thunder god, ruled the storms and tempests. With eyes ablaze and hair aflame, he bears his red-hot hammer in its iron gauntlet. As his bronze chariot made a racket like the clash and clatter of copper kettles, he was nicknamed the Kettle Vendor. (ILLUSTRATION BY JAMES ALEXANDER, 1995.)

thrusting it upwards. Then the frost giant returned and tried to kill Thor as well. Using a pair of tongs, he launched a red-hot iron ball at Thor, but the thunder god caught it deftly in the iron gloves he had been given by Grid, and returned the compliment by throwing it back at the giant. The iron ball passed through an iron pillar before tearing a hole in Geirrod's belly. Afterwards Thor smashed the skulls of all the servants.

The frost giant mentioned by Grid, the powerful Hrungnir, had fallen in single combat with Thor. Foolishly, the frost giant challenged Odin to a horse race but then, as a guest at the gods' stronghold of ASGARD, he drank too much and insulted the gods. When Thor returned at this point the giant challenged Thor to a duel.

The frost giants did what they could to aid Hrungnir in the forthcoming fight. They built a clay giant

annoyance. "You should not give a horse to the son of a giantess instead of your own father," complained Odin.

Another famous adventure in Jotunheim concerns the visit of Thor and Loki to the stronghold of *UTGARD*. On the way the thunder god passed through Midgard, the land of people, and gained two human servants named *THIALFI* and *ROSKVA*, a brother and sister. It happened that Thialfi disobeyed an instruction of Thor when they dined together at his parents' farm. Thor told everyone to be careful with the bones of some goats they were eating. But hungry Thialfi split a thigh bone to get at the marrow, before throwing the bone on the goat skins in a corner. Next morning, when Thor used his magic hammer to restore the eaten goats to life, the thunder god noticed that one of them was lame. As compensation and in order to prevent him from slaying the household, Thialfi and Roskva pledged themselves as Thor's servants.

As Thor, Loki, Thialfi and Roskva neared Utgard, they spent one night in an empty hall. It was so big that several of the halls in Asgard, the home of the gods, could have fitted inside it at the same time. Later they realized that the hall was in fact the thumb of a frost giant's empty glove. It belonged to *SKRYMIR*, whose name means "vast". Blows delivered by a frustrated Thor to Skrymir's sleeping head were dismissed by the giant as either a leaf or a twig brushing his brow during the night. On their arrival at Utgard, the travellers were just as amazed at the stronghold's dimensions. While Thor

said that size was of no importance – "the bigger they are, the heavier they fall" – Loki was more thoughtful. Inside Utgard huge frost giants eyed the four guests. Their leader at first ignored them, but finally acknowledged "little" Thor. Then he devised a series of games in which Loki, Thialfi and Thor all

failed to shine. First the fire god lost an eating contest. A second event saw Thialfi easily outpaced in a foot-race. Then successively Thor lost a drinking contest, managed to lift only one paw of a cat, and, most embarrassing of all, was easily wrestled down on to one knee by "an old, old woman".

Once Thor admitted on leaving Utgard that they had come off second best, the leader of the frost giants revealed that he had used spells to gain the advantage. He told them how Loki had actually been pitted against wildfire, and Thialfi against his own thought, while Thor had tried to swallow the ocean, lift the massive sea serpent Jormungand and wrestle with old age. As soon as this message was delivered, Utgard vanished. Only then did it dawn on Thor that Skrymir and Utgard were illusions, vast creations sent out by frightened frost giants. But it gave Loki some satisfaction to learn that brain had indeed triumphed over brawn.

Even Thor had to admit that on certain occasions Loki's cleverness was necessary to hold the frost giants in check. Such a moment in time was when Mjollnir, Thor's magic hammer, fell into their hands after it was stolen by the dwarfs. Its new owner, the frost giant THRYM, demanded as the price of the hammer's return the hand of FREYJA, the fertility goddess. Loki got Thor to dress in Freyja's clothes and go to Thrym's hall instead. Despite his god-like appetite, Thor was passed

THOR (above) impulsive as ever, confronted mighty Skrymir with his tiny hammer, bashing him over the head to silence his snores, but to no avail. Each time the giant woke he scratched his brow and nodded off again. Later, Thor learnt that Skrymir had been an illusion. (ILLUSTRATION BY J HUARD, 1930.)

THOR (left) and his party visited the icy citadel of Utgard, the stronghold of the frost giants, where they underwent a series of allegorical tests. Thialfi was outstripped by the speed of Thought, Loki out-eaten by Wildfire, and Thor overcome by Age. Here, Thor fails to drain a horn brimful of the ocean. (ILLUSTRATION BY JAMES ALEXANDER, 1995.)

THOR (above) wrestles with Jormungand in their final combat at Ragnarok. Trapped within the serpent's crushing coils, Thor smashed its ugly head with a fatal blow of his hammer; he then staggered back nine paces and drowned in the flood of venom flowing from the beast's gaping jaws. (ILLUSTRATION BY JAMES ALEXANDER, 1995.)

off by his "bridesmaid" Loki as a blushing bride, and an excited Thrym handed over Mjollnir. The ensuing massacre did a great deal to restore Thor's fierce reputation, which had been tarnished by the god having to dress like a woman.

Mjollnir was the sole protection of the gods against the frost giants. It was the thunderbolt which terrorized them prior to the catastrophe of Ragnarok. Apart from its destructive side, the hammer had other magic powers over fertility and death. It seems to have had the ability to restore animal life. It also hallowed marriage, for otherwise Thrym would not have been so ready to place Mjollnir between

Thor's knees when the thunder god was disguised as Freyja. But throughout the myths relating to Thor we are never unconscious of its unlimited destructive powers. For it was the thunder god's purpose to quell the enemies of the gods – "to smash their legs, break their skulls, and crush their backs". Like his Hindu equivalent Indra, Thor was the scourge of evil and in Germanic mythology this could only mean frost giants. Loki's eventual siding with these grim opponents is therefore one of the saddest events to befall Thor, for the two gods "both enjoyed each other's company". (See also NORSE HEROES; RAGNAROK)

RINGS OF POWER

AMONG THE VIKINGS, the ring was a potent symbol of power, fortune and fame. A gift of honour and form of currency, it was also sometimes a royal heirloom, such as the Swedish Sviagriss. The magical rings of Norse myth were also symbols of destiny and, in their bleakest form, symbols of doom. One famous example was the cursed ring, Andvarinaut, which blighted many lives. Another ring of doom was Thor's Domhring, formed by a circle of stone statues surrounding a punishment pillar in front of his temple. The Domhring possibly symbolized the inevitability of retribution. Much more joyous and fabulous rings were Odin's astounding Draupnir which literally dripped eight similar gold rings every nine days; or Thor's Oath Ring, a symbol of fair play and good faith. The rings of heroes inevitably brought wealth and power, but not always happiness and sometimes tragedy, if corrupted by greed. Yet the pure rings of Orthnit, Wolfdietrich and Dietrich were symbols of a ring-lord's circle of power and everlasting fame.

DRAUPNIR,

Odin's fabulous ring,

was an emblem of abundance

and power. Precious beyond compare, it

dripped eight similar gold rings every ninth night, consolidating his vast wealth and dominion over the nine worlds. Draupnir was crafted by the dwarf, Sindri, while his brother, Brokk, pumped the bellows. In an extravagant gesture of grief, Odin cast the ring upon Balder's funeral pyre, but later retrieved it when Hermod ventured to Hel. The return of the ring symbolized the promise of fertility after winter bleakness. Here, the dwarf Sindri fashions the magnificent ring with fire and arcane magic in his underground forge. (ILLUSTRATION BY ALAN LEE, 1984.)

THE GOLD RING among the Vikings was a precious token of power, fame and fortune. Sometimes bequeathed as an heirloom, it was also often buried with the ring-lord for the journey to the otherworld, such as this burial treasure. Exquisitely wrought, the ring's clear, bold lines express the vigour and strength of Viking craft.

(GILT SILVER, 10TH CENTURY.)

ALBERICH (above), a dwarf of the Niebelungenlied, forged a ring of power from the Rhinegold stolen from the Rhine Maidens. News of the gold robbery and ring of power incited gods and giants alike to action. The giants Fafner and Fasolt demanded the ring in payment for building Valhalla, and carried off Freyja as a hostage. In the border, the gods, Odin, Frigg, Loki, Freyr and Thor all search despairingly for the hidden treasure. (ILLUSTRATION BY F VON STASSEN, 1914.)

DIETRICH (above), a Gothic hero, won a wondrous ring from the dwarf, Laurin, who ruled a fabulous underground kingdom lit by gems. After various battles and intrigues, Dietrich overcame the wily dwarf, and claimed his magical gold ring as well as a girdle of strength, a cape of invisibility, a magical sword and a vast ring-hoard. Laurin's ring was the very one owned by Dietrich's great-grandfather, the Emperor Wolfdietrich. Here, Dietrich breaks into Laurin's enchanted, ever-flowering rose garden, before winning the ring treasures. (ILLUSTRATION BY ALAN LEE, 1984.)

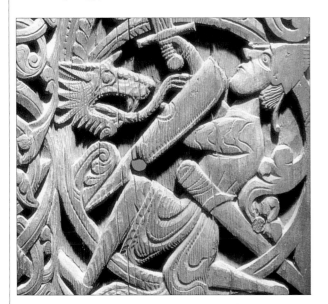

SIGURD (right) won the cursed ring, Andvarinaut, after slaying its dragon guardian, Fafnir. Although innocent himself, he suffered from the ring's web of doom. After falling in love with the splendid Valkyrie, Brynhild, he was bewitched by Grimhild into betraying Brynhild by marrying Gudrun. When his memory returned, he suffered from guilt and grief. Sigurd's gold in turn evoked the envy of the Nibelung brothers who slew him, urged on by a vengeful Brynhild, seeking to assuage her honour. As the hero breathed his last, he died calling to Brynhild. (ILLUSTRATION BY ARTHUR RACKHAM, C. 1900.)

THE RING ANDVARINAUT wove a fortune of gold much like Draupnir, but was tainted by the bitter curse of Andvari. Heidmar, who had demanded the ring as wiergold from Loki, was the first to suffer from the curse by falling at the hands of his son, Fafnir, who lusted after the gold. Next, Fafnir turned himself into a monstrous dragon to guard the ring-hoard. When the youthful hero Sigurd (above) slew the dragon, he inherited the fabulous ring-hoard, but with it a terrible curse. (WOOD CARVING, 12TH CENTURY.)

T

THRUD, in Germanic mythology, was the daughter of the thunder god *THOR* and his wife *SIF*. She was promised to the dwarf *ALVIS* as a payment for his handicraft. But Thor prevented the dwarf from claiming Thrud by keeping him talking until morning, when the sunlight turned Alvis into stone.

THRYM, in Germanic mythology, was the frost giant who came to acquire *THOR*'s magic hammer. The gods were at a loss because only this weapon could protect them against the frost giants. When Thrym said he would exchange the hammer for the fertility goddess *FREYJA*, the fire god *LOKI* persuaded Thor to go to the frost giant's stronghold disguised as the bride in order to recover the hammer. Loki also went along in the form of a maidservant. Thus the unusual pair arrived at Thrym's hall. Even though the frost giant was quite suspicious about his bride-to-be, Loki cleverly managed to talk him into producing the hammer, which Thor then used to lay low all the frost giants in sight.

THRYM (left), a daring storm giant, stole Thor's sacred hammer, causing panic at Asgard. Here, the giant broods on his rocky hilltop overlooked by Loki, disguised as a falcon, and scouting the icy wastes in search of the hammer, buried eight fathoms down. (ILLUSTRATION BY JAMES ALEXANDER, 1995.)

TIR see *TYR*

TIWAZ see *TYR*

TRIGLAV was a three-headed god of the Slavs living in central Europe. At Stettin in present-day Poland, Triglav once boasted four separate temples. These were maintained by war booty, one tenth being the amount due to the god at the end of a campaign. The best temple at Stettin housed a black horse for Triglav's use. In the twelfth century Christianity arrived and Triglav's statues were broken and their multiple heads sent to the Pope in Rome as curiosities.

TUONI was the Finnish god of the dead, who lived in the dark land of Tuonela, from which few travellers return. With his wife Tuonetar he had several children who were deities of suffering, including Kipu-Tytto, goddess of illness. One of the few heroes who managed to escape from Tuonela was *VAINAMOINEN*. After successfully crossing the river that marked the border of Tuonela, he was received there by Tuonetar, who gave him beer to drink. But while her visitor slept, her son created a vast iron mesh across the river so that Vainamoinen could not return that way and would be trapped forever. But when he woke, the hero changed into an otter and swam easily through the net.

TUONI guarded the dark realm of Tuonela on the banks of a black river. When Vainamoinen visited Tuoni in search of magic charms, he was trapped by a vast iron net, flung across the river; but the hero changed into an otter and slipped through. (ILLUSTRATION BY NICK BEALE, 1995.)

TYR (left), famed for his bravery and might, was assigned the task of feeding Fenrir, the fierce wolf-son of Loki. Yet Fenrir kept on growing, stronger and fiercer every day, until all-seeing Odin realized the danger and the gods decided to bind the beast underground. (ILLUSTRATION BY J HUARD, 1930.)

TYR (above left), a popular sword god, was invoked before battle, honoured with sword dances, and had his rune engraved on blades. He lost his right hand in a fight with Fenrir, but was just as skilful with his left, and at Ragnarok slew the hell-hound Garm. (ILLUSTRATION BY JAMES ALEXANDER, 1995.)

URD (above), a wise Norn, personified the past, while her sisters represented present and future fate. The Norns warned the gods of future evil and drew lessons from the past. Urd fed two swans on the Urdar pool who gave birth to the swans of the world. (ILLUSTRATION BY JAMES ALEXANDER, 1995.)

TYR, also known as Tiv and Tiwaz, was the Germanic war god, and the son of *ODIN* and his wife *FRIGG*. The Anglo-Saxons usually called him Tiw and gave his name to Tuesday (Tiwesdaeg in Old English). He was closely associated with Odin and, like that god, received sacrifices of hanged men. It is not unlikely that Tyr was an early sky god whose powers were later passed to Odin and Thor. *GUNGNIR*, Odin's magic spear, may once have belonged to Tyr, since it was customary for the Vikings to cast a spear over the heads of an enemy as a sacrifice before fighting commenced in earnest, and over recent years archaeologists have found numerous splendidly ornamented spears dedicated to Tyr.

The myth of Tyr relates to the binding of the wolf *FENRIR*. This monstrous creature had grown so powerful that the gods decided to restrain it. No ordinary chain was strong enough, and before Fenrir would consent to a magic one being placed round his neck, Tyr had to put his hand in the wolf's mouth as a sign of goodwill. When the wolf discovered the chain could not be broken, he bit off Tyr's hand. Although Tyr was in agony, the other gods just laughed. The downgrading of Tyr may not be unconnected with the loss of a hand. A Celtic god by the name of Nuada was forced to give up the leadership of the Irish Tuatha De Danann ("the people of the goddess Dana") after he lost a hand at the first battle of Magh Tuireadh. But Tyr was still able to fight at *RAGNAROK*, during which it was destined that the hound Garm, which stood at the gates of *HEL*, acting as watchdog to the land of the dead, was to leap at Tyr's throat and they would kill each other.

URD, or Wyrd (meaning "Fate" or "Past"), was one of three sisters who were the Germanic fates and were known as the *NORNS*. The two other sisters were Verdandi ("Being" or "Present") and Skuld ("Necessity" or "Future"). Urd gave her name to the well that was situated beneath one of the roots of *YGGDRASIL*, the cosmic tree, and that was where the gods would hold their daily meeting. As was also the case in Greek mythology, the gods were not superior or beyond the influence of the fates. Indeed, Urd warned the chief of the Germanic gods, *ODIN*, that he was destined to be killed by the terrible wolf *FENRIR* at *RAGNAROK*, the doom of the gods.

V

UTGARD ("Outer Place"), in Germanic mythology, was the huge giants' stronghold in *JOTUNHEIM*, where *LOKI*, *THOR* and Thor's servant *THIALFI* found themselves in contests against unequal opponents. Loki failed to consume more food than wildfire; Thialfi could not keep pace as a runner with thought; and Thor was unable to drink the sea dry, pick up the sea serpent *JORMUNGAND* or wrestle old age. When they left, the gods realized that Utgard was an illusion made by the frightened frost giants to deter Thor, their greatest enemy.

VAFTHRUDNIR, in Germanic mythology, was a wise frost giant. He was believed to have gained his impressive store of wisdom by consulting the dead. Possibly like *ODIN*, the chief of the gods, who voluntarily hanged himself for nine nights on *YGGDRASIL*, the cosmic tree, in order to become wise, Vafthrudnir had also temporarily died. Seeking to test his knowledge against the giant's, Odin decided to journey to Vafthrudnir's land in disguise. There he challenged the gigantic "riddle-master" to match their knowledge of the past, the present and the future. After an impressive display on the part of both Odin and Vafthrudnir, the giant was eventually defeated by a quite unanswerable question, when the god asked the giant what he had whispered to his dead son *BALDER* before he lit the pyre on which he lay. It is implied in the story that Odin's foreknowledge allowed him to assure Balder of future resurrection and worship on the new earth, "risen out of the water, fresh and green", after *RAGNAROK*, the doom of the gods and the end of the world.

UTGARD, the icy citadel of the frost giants, was carved out of snow blocks and glittering icicles. The Norse poets, who knew all about the terrors of the ice of their northern homes, inevitably portrayed the evil giants in just such a harsh realm, where numbing cold froze the muscles and paralysed the will. (ILLUSTRATION BY ALAN LEE, 1984.)

Now Vafthrudnir recognized Odin and admitted that no one could tell what the god had whispered into the ear of the dead Balder. The frost giant's last words were: "So I have pitted myself against Odin, always the wisest."

VAINAMOINEN, the chief hero of Finnish epic, was the son of a primal goddess, *LUONNOTAR*. He was always depicted as a vigorous and sensitive old man, who from birth possessed the wisdom of the ages, for he was in his mother's womb for at least thirty years. As the champion of the Kalevala (which means "the fatherland of heroes"), Vainamoinen was gifted with extraordinary magical powers. He was less lucky in love, however. When he sought a bride from among the women of Pohja, he was promised one of Louhi's daughters if he made the magic talisman, the Sampo. He gave the task to his comrade Ilmarinen and so Louhi's daughter was married to Ilmarinen instead. But the bride was killed and the magic talisman stolen, so Vainamoinen and Ilmarinen, joined by *LEMINKAINEN*, set off to find the Sampo. After several great adventures, they succeeded in recovering it. However, Louhi raised a great storm and, in the form of a griffin, descended onto their ship. Only the swift action of Vainamoinen saved them, but during the storm the Sampo was lost to the winds. When the storm had passed, Vainamoinen collected all the scattered pieces together and was able to restore some of the talisman's former power. With his mission completed, Vainamoinen built a ship and embarked on an endless voyage. (See also *TREASURES AND TALISMANS; SORCERY AND SPELLS*)

VAINAMOINEN (above), a peerless mage, was also a gentle, humane hero. A tireless explorer, he journeyed across the known world and, alone among heroes, returned from the underworld. At the end of his life, he set sail in a copper boat and embarked on a voyage without end. (VAINOMOINEN BY A GALLEN-KALLELA, CANVAS, C. 1890.)

VAINAMOINEN (below) courts reluctant Aino in her father's grove. Promised to the old man against her will by her brother, she drowned herself rather than marry, only to wind up as a salmon on his fishing line, before leaping back into the river and returning to her human form. (THE AINO TRIPTYCH BY A GALLEN-KALLELA, CANVAS, C. 1890.)

The newly fallen joining the residents in Valhalla had to enter by a door called Valgrind ("the sacred barred-gate of the slain"). Even before they reached this entrance, they must pass several obstacles, including a fast-running river of air. Once in Valhalla "the men killed in war" were miraculously cured of their wounds and were able to indulge endlessly in the pleasures of feasting and fighting. The meat of a magic boar was prepared as wonderful stew in an inexhaustible cauldron. The same boar was eaten day after day through a process of resurrection. Mead was provided from the teats of a goat. It was said that every day the Einherjar put on their armour, went to the practice ground and fought each other. If killed, they were restored to life. At midday they returned to Valhalla and started drinking. Such an existence for a Viking helps to explain Odin's popularity in Denmark, southern Norway and Sweden, the regions where most of the raiding expeditions came from.

VALHALLA'S Valkyries – beautiful battle-maidens – welcomed the chosen slain with open arms. At other times, Odin's sons, Hermod or Bragi, received the heroes, conducting them to the foot of Odin's throne; while Odin himself rose to greet the bravest Vikings at the gate. (ILLUSTRATION BY E WALLCOUSINS, C. 1920.)

VALHALLA was a Viking's paradise where chosen heroes fought and feasted from dawn to dusk. Wounds healed overnight, and mead and meat flowed freely. The hectic round of combat ensured that heroes stayed in fighting form, fit for the final battle at Ragnarok. (ILLUSTRATION BY W B DRACK, 1900.)

VALHALLA (above), the Hall of the Slain, was built in the shimmering grove of Glesir. Encircled by strong outer walls, the magnificent hall glittered with precious metals, its walls were built of spears and its roof of shining shields. This starlit scene evokes a sense of the untold wonders that lie within. (ILLUSTRATION BY F VON STASSEN, 1914.)

VALHALLA, or Valholl, in Germanic mythology, was the hall of the *EINHERJAR* ("heroic dead"), those warriors slain on the battle-field and chosen by *ODIN* himself as his followers. Built in *ASGARD* by Odin, Valhalla was enormous. It had over five hundred doors, each wide enough to allow up to eight hundred men to march through abreast. These wide doors were designed to allow the chosen war-riors to pour forth at the first sign of *RAGNAROK*, the doom of the gods. Then they were destined to fall again, alongside the gods, in a great battle on the *VIGRID* Plain.

Odin was known as the father of the slain and he was the host who presided over Valhalla, and daily sent out the *VALKYRIES* to add to the number of the dead. In Valhalla the Valkyries would carry food and drinks for the Einherjar.

Ragnarok was always given as the reason for creating Valhalla. When asked about his habit of giving luck to a warrior in a battle and then suddenly taking it away, Odin said that "the grey wolf watches the halls of the gods": that is to say, the gods were constantly threatened by Ragnarok, the catastrophe in which they would die in mutual destruction with the frost giants and the forces of evil. The gathering of the "heroic dead" in Valhalla was the only way the gods could prepare to face their own fate, no matter how vain the attempt would prove to be. At least Odin's men, caught up in a berserk fury, could be guaranteed to tear into the enemy ranks in one last battle. (See also *THE VALKYRIES*)

VALHOLL see *VALHALLA*

VALI was one of the few bright young gods to survive Ragnarok. Destined from birth to avenge Balder's death, he grew at an amazing rate, reaching manhood in a single day and rushing off with uncombed hair to slay Hodr. Here, he is portrayed striding across the new earth after Ragnarok. (ILLUSTRATION BY NICK BEALE, 1995.)

VALI was the son of *ODIN* and *RIND* and was destined to kill blind *HODR* in revenge for his unwitting murder of *BALDER*. Fulfilling a prophecy, he grew from a baby to manhood in a single day and rushed off to kill Hodr. Along with his half-brother *VIDAR*, he survived *RAGNAROK*. Another Vali was one of the unlucky sons of *LOKI*.

THE VALKYRIES ("female choosers of the slain") were *ODIN*'s battle- or shield-maidens. They rode over battlefields and selected the *EINHERJAR* ("heroic dead") who would go to *VALHALLA*. They probably derived from something more dreadful than the attendants of Valhalla, and must have originally been the goddesses of slaughter itself, wild Amazon-like creatures who took great delight in the severed limbs and bloody wounds of battle. Something of this early terror can be imagined in an account of the battle of Stamford Bridge, King Harold's victory over the Norwegians shortly before his defeat by the Normans at Battle in 1066. A soldier in the Norwegian army dreamt of a Valkyrie before the battle. He thought he was on the king of Norway's ship, when he beheld a great witch on an island, with a fork in one hand to rake up the dead and a trough in the other to catch the blood. (See also *THE VALKYRIES*; *RAGNAROK*)

VALKYRIES (above), Odin's martial maidens, alighted on the battlefield to select the bravest warriors for Valhalla, the idyllic abode of Odin's ghostly army. Although quite charming in Valhalla, on the battlefield the Valkyries became sinister spirits of slaughter, goading heroes to their death. (THE VALKYRIES BY G VON LEEKE, 1870.)

VALKYRIES (below) rode through the stormy sky on magnificent pearly steeds, personifying clouds, and whose soaking manes sprayed the earth with fertile frost and dew. They also scoured the seas, snatching sailors from ships, or sometimes beckoning from the strand. (THE RIDE OF THE VALKYRIE BY H HERMAN, CANVAS, C. 1890.)

RAGNAROK

RAGNAROK WAS THE preordained doom of the gods, and the climax of the cosmic drama. The seeds of doom were sown at the dawn of time when the world and its first creatures emerged from the violent extremes of ice and fire. Inherently fragile, the universe was beset by forces of destruction and flawed from the outset. The inevitable climax was precipitated by a series of disasters. Loki, a catalyst of evil, spawned three fearsome monsters against whom the gods were ultimately powerless. Consumed with hate, Loki went on to slay Balder, symbol of goodness and beauty. Beyond Asgard, the enmity of the hostile giants gathered momentum until, at Ragnarok, all the world's destructive forces burst forth in cataclysmic disaster. Apocalypse is a common mythical theme, but the Norse vision is starker than most and unique in the loss of its gods. In one hopeful version, some gods survive and the earth emerges fresh and green, purged by flood and fire. Ragnarok casts a dark shadow over the Norse myths, yet also highlights the heroism of gods and heroes.

LOKI (left), ever envious of anyone who was good and beautiful, guided blind Hodr to slay his brother, Balder, with a dart of mistletoe. The wanton destruction of the best of the gods marked a turning-point in Loki's downward spiral of evil. Yet even after the crime, the gods allowed Loki to roam unrestrained, growing ever more bitter and twisted. (LOKI AND HODR BY C QVARNSTROM, MARBLE, C. 1890.)

THE MIGHT OF THOR (above) and his hammer, Mjollnir, symbolized the foremost defence of the gods against the threat of the giants and the doom of Ragnarok. Yet Thor's sustained might proved ultimately inadequate to withstand the combined onslaught of giants and monsters. At the end, however, Thor rid the world of the giant monster, Jormungand, before dying himself from its venom. (THOR BY B FOGELBERG, MARBLE, C. 1890.)

JORMUNGAND (above) was one of the evils threatening the survival of the Norse world. Along with his monster siblings, Fenrir and Hel, Jormungand epitomized darkness and destruction. The massive serpent lurked in the ocean depths, circling the world in a stranglehold. Coiled in upon itself, this striking snake motif recalls the World Serpent curled around Midgard with its tail in its mouth, until it burst forth at Ragnarok. (BROOCH, 7TH CENTURY.)

LOKI (above) gate-crashes Aegir's feast and ridicules the gods with his sardonic wit, undermining and humiliating each in turn. None can either match or silence him, until Thor enters and threatens Loki with his hammer. Odin, at the right, looks on in speechless sorrow, recognizing the signs of Ragnarok. (AEGIR'S FEAST BY C HANSEN, CANVAS, C. 1861.)

ODIN (left), despite all his wisdom and power, was powerless to prevent the imminent doom of the gods. Yet he tried everything to fend off the fateful moment. Here, he carves magic runes on his spear, setting out rules of conduct for giants and dwarfs, gods and mortals. Odin learnt the wisdom of the runes from the dead when hanging from the sacred Yggdrasil in voluntary self-sacrifice. He also paid for wisdom with one eye at Mimir's well. Yet all his spies and sources only reinforce his own foreknowledge of doom. (ILLUSTRATION BY F VON STASSEN, 1914.)

AT RAGNAROK (above) the mighty walls of Asgard, home of the Aesir gods, were destroyed and the heavenly Bifrost Bridge was set alight by Surt, the fearsome flame giant. Jormungand, the gigantic World Serpent, burst from the seething ocean and engulfed the Vigrid Plain, spewing venom in all directions. Fenrir broke his bonds and roamed the earth with his savage brood, spreading death and destruction. The wolves swallowed the sun and moon, and even Yggdrasil itself shuddered. Over the whirling seas, Loki sailed with his giant host, while his daughter Hel rose from misty Niflheim with her pale army of the dead, and the assembled host issued forth over the Vigrid Plain. At the very end, Surt set all the nine worlds ablaze and the earth sank beneath the boiling ocean. (ILLUSTRATION BY ALAN LEE, 1984.)

THE VALKYRIES (left), Odin's formidable martial shield-maidens, gathered up the heroic slain from the battlefield and ferried them to Valhalla where they kept in fighting form until Ragnarok. By raising a heroic army, Odin determined to put up a fighting stand against the enemy host at Ragnarok. (THE RIDE OF THE VALKYRIES ANON.)

THE VANIR were the older of the two branches of the Germanic family of gods and were fertility deities. They lived at Vanaheim, far from ASGARD, the fortified residence of the AESIR, the younger branch, who were primarily war gods. Myth relates how the Vanir and the Aesir fought for supremacy not long after creation. After the Aesir had won, peace was sealed by an exchange of gods and goddesses. The Vanir sent to Asgard the sea god NJORD and his twin son and daughter FREYR and FREYJA, and also KVASIR, who was believed to be second to none in his wisdom. The Aesir despatched to Vanaheim long-legged HONIR and wise MIMIR.

At first Honir and Mimir were welcomed and accepted by the Vanir, but the gods gradually came to the conclusion that they had got the worst of the exchange with the Aesir. The problem was the terrible indecisiveness of Honir, which reached embarrassing proportions whenever Mimir was absent. To the Vanir it seemed that Mimir was not only Honir's voice but also his brain, so in anger they cut off Mimir's head and sent it back to Asgard. Although this did not rekindle the conflict, it effectively caused a rift between the Aesir and the Vanir which greatly reduced the mythological significance of the Vanir, so they slowly faded into the background.

The distinction between the older Vanir and the younger Aesir was uncertain even in Viking times. When the sagas were collected in the late twelfth century, there was speculation about the origins of the two groups. The Icelander Snorri Sturluson thought that the name of the Aesir recalled their homeland in Asia, and that THOR was the grandson of King Priam of Troy and ODIN his descendant in the twentieth generation, while the Vanir were originally inhabitants of the land by the River Don, formerly called Vanaquisl. Today, however, these theories have been discounted.

THE VANIR, deities of fertility, wealth and health, were worshipped by farmers. The three main Vanir gods, Njord (centre) and his lovely twins, Freyja and Freyr, were all gentle, benign spirits of nature, who nourished the earth and seas, and granted fair weather and good harvests. (ILLUSTRATION BY JAMES ALEXANDER, 1995.)

VE, in Germanic mythology, was one of the sons of BOR and the brother of ODIN and VILI. At the beginning of creation the primeval cow AUDHUMLA sustained herself by licking the ice and from her ample teats flowed enough milk to feed the frost giant YMIR, the first living creature. He is described as being utterly evil. However, Audhumla's licking also uncovered BURI, the grand-father of Ve. All the gods were descended from Buri, because his son Bor married the frost giantess Bestla and had three sons – Odin, Vili and Ve.

Although the blood of the frost giants and the gods intermingled, the implacable enmity between them could not be denied or resolved, for it went right back to the killing of Ymir. Odin, Vili and Ve disliked Ymir and his growing band of frost giants. Eventually, their dislike turned to hatred and they slew Ymir, making the world in GINNUNGAGAP (the "yawning emptiness") from the giant's body.

Afterwards the three brothers found on the seashore two fallen trees, an ash and an elm. From the wood they made first man and then woman. Odin breathed into them the spirit of life; Vili gave them intelligence and emotion; and Ve added the ability to see and hear. In some versions of the creation myth, Ve is known as Lodur or Lothur.

THE VANIR were famed for magic and foresight of which the macho Aesir were a little suspicious, except for Odin who, ever eager to increase his knowledge, rapidly absorbed the Vanir arts. Here, the fruitful Vanir twins follow Odin and Frigg over the Bifrost Bridge, with Thor and Loki in the rear. (ILLUSTRATION BY F VON STASSEN, 1914.)

VIDAR (above), a strong, silent and solitary god, lived alone in a leafy palace deep in his primal forest. He personified the imperishable forces of nature, and was one of the few gods destined to survive Ragnarok. He slew the wolf Fenrir with his iron-shod foot.

(ILLUSTRATION BY NICK BEALE, 1995.)

VE (above) and his brothers, Vili and Odin, fashioned human forms from two pieces of driftwood lying on the cosmic beach at the dawn of time. Odin created a man from the ash, while his younger brothers formed a woman from the elm, and then Odin breathed life into them.

(ILLUSTRATION BY JAMES ALEXANDER, 1995.)

VELES guarded cattle and flocks for the Slavs. Especially popular with farmers, he survived into the nineteenth century, when Russian farmers still honoured him in the harvest fields by curling the ears of one sheaf of corn (see right), symbolizing the god's curly hair and beard.

(ILLUSTRATION BY NICK BEALE, 1995.)

VELES, or Volos, was the Russian god who had authority over flocks and herds. It was customary to swear oaths in the names of Veles and *PERUNU*, who was the thunder god. When Vladimir, ruler of Kiev, was baptized into the Orthodox faith in 988, he had a statue of Veles thrown into the River Dniepner. In Russian folklore, however, the god of flocks survives. For instance, at harvest time the ears of the last sheaf of corn are still

woven into a plait known as "Veles' beard". Also in Russian Orthodox tradition, Veles was incorporated into the Christian faith by identifying him with St Blasius, who was a shepherd and martyr from Cappadocia. Prayers offered to this saint are expected to protect and increase flocks of sheep and goats.

VIDAR was the silent and solitary god of Germanic mythology. He was the son of *ODIN* and the frost giantess *GRID*, and lived in a place called Vidi, where all was quiet and peaceful. It was Vidar's destiny to avenge his father's death at *RAGNAROK*, the doom of the gods and the end of the world. When the terrible wolf *FENRIR* had overcome Odin in a fierce and bloody struggle and swallowed him, Vidar stepped forward, smashed one of his well-shod feet against the wolf's lower jaw, and then with both hands he forced the upper jaw open till the ravenous beast's throat was torn asunder. It is more than likely that the meaning of Vidar's own name refers in some way to this ripping in half of evil.

V

VIGRID, in Germanic mythology, was the name of a plain that was destined to be the scene of the final conflict between the gods and the frost giants. There at *RAGNAROK* the two sides and their allies would engage in mutual destruction. A huge expanse of land, Vigrid was said to stretch 120 leagues in every direction. Even so, it was predicted that the assembled hosts would cover it completely.

VILI, in Germanic mythology, was the son of *BOR* and Bestla and the brother of *ODIN* and *VE*. At the beginning of creation he helped his brothers to slay the frost giant *YMIR* and form the world from his carcass. When they later created the first man and woman from wood, Vili's contribution was sharp wits and feeling hearts. Odin gave them the breath of life, while Ve added the powers of sight and hearing. In one Icelandic poem Vili is given the name *HONIR*.

VLKODLAK was the Slavic wolfman. More a figure of folklore than mythology, he exists because of the ancient respect accorded to the ravenous wolf, which in the forests of northern and eastern Europe was the animal most feared. According to Germanic mythology, the chief god *ODIN* was destined to be killed by the wolf *FENRIR* at *RAGNAROK*, the doom of the gods.

VOLOS see *VELES*

VOLSUNG was the subject of a late Germanic myth. He was said to be a descendant of *ODIN*. When Signy, Volsung's only daughter, was married against her will to the Gothic king Siggeir, a one-eyed stranger appeared among the wedding guests. It was Odin, chief of the Germanic gods. He stuck a sword deep into an oak and told the company that the weapon would belong to the man who pulled it out. Whoever wielded the sword could never be defeated.

THE VIGRID PLAIN (above) was mapped out as the battlefield of Ragnarok. When Heimdall sounded the call to battle, the warring hosts converged from all corners of the earth; gods and heroes poured over the Bifrost Bridge, while Loki and the fiery host swarmed in from the swirling seas.
(ILLUSTRATION BY JAMES ALEXANDER, 1995.)

Out of courtesy Volsung invited his son-in-law Siggeir to try his luck first. But Siggeir did not succeed. Nor was anyone else able to pull out the sword, except the youngest of Volsung's sons, Sigmund. When Siggeir offered to buy the magic weapon, Sigmund refused to part with it at any price.

This refusal made the Gothic king really angry. Despite Signy's

VOLSUNG'S (below) great hall, built around a sacred oak, was the scene of a magical event when Odin appeared one night and thrust a sword, hilt-deep, into the great oak. He challenged the heroes to pull it out, offering the divine gift to the winner. Sigmund was the much-envied champion.
(ILLUSTRATION BY ALAN LEE, 1984.)

warning, Volsung and his ten sons walked into Siggeir's trap when they accepted an invitation to visit his court. They were ambushed on the way and left in the forest, bound to a fallen tree. Each night a wolf came and ate one of them, until only Sigmund was left alive. Signy succeeded in rescuing him.

As a result, Siggeir wrongly believed that no one had escaped the attentions of the wolf. He relaxed his guard and Signy was able to bury her family and help Sigmund. It took a long time to prepare a revenge, however. First of all Signy tried to have her own sons trained by Sigmund, but they lacked courage. A second attempt to reinforce her brother involved incest. Without his knowledge, Signy slept with him and bore Sinfiotli, a warrior with double Volsung blood. When Sinfiotli grew up, Signy sent him to her brother to be trained as a warrior.

Although Sigmund and Sinfiotli were captured by Siggeir, the magic sword secured their release and allowed them to take revenge on the king and his sons. Afterwards Sigmund returned home, and had another son, *SIGURD*, known in German legend as Siegfried.

VOLUND see *WAYLAND*

WAYLAND was the smith god of the Anglo-Saxons. The son of a sailor and a mermaid, he was renowned for making coats of mail and swords. In Scandinavia he was known as Volund, or Volundr, and in Germany as Wielund.

Wayland's myth is a story of revenge. King Nidud of Sweden cut Wayland's leg sinews and placed him and his forge on a remote island. The smith god avenged this mutilation by killing Nidud's two sons, who came to see his treasures, and sending their heads studded with precious jewels and mounted on silver to King Nidud. He may also have raped Nidud's daughter, but this is not certain.

WAYLAND's (above) smithy was visited not just by warriors seeking arms, but by noblewomen wanting dainty trinkets of purest gold. Wayland was also a craftsman on the grand scale, designing a fabulous Icelandic maze, known as Volund's House. (WHALEBONE CARVING, 8TH CENTURY.)

WAYLAND (below), captive on a desolate island, laboured in his underground forge, fashioning wondrous ornaments and weapons for his oppressive master, Nidud of Sweden. Like Daedalus, Wayland fashioned wings and flew away to freedom. (WIELAND BY MAX KOCH, WATERCOLOUR, 1904.)

WAYLAND (above right) and his brothers chanced upon three Valkyries bathing in a lake. They took their plumage left on the bank and kept them on earth for nine years, until they escaped. Fashioning wings for himself, Wayland flew after his wife, Alvit, to Alfheim. (ILLUSTRATION BY H THEAKER, 1900.)

Afterwards Wayland is said to have flown to *VALHALLA*, like the Greek inventor Daedalus, on wings he had made for himself. Near Uffington in Wiltshire, a long barrow has ancient associations with Wayland, and is locally known as his smithy. His lameness parallels that of Hephaistos, the Greek smith god whose injury had two different explanations. In one version it was claimed that his limp was the result of his having interfered in a violent quarrel between his parents, Zeus and Hera. So annoyed did Zeus become that he flung his son out of Olympus and let him fall heavily on the island of Lemnos. A second explanation tells how Hephaistos was born a dwarfish figure with a limp. Hera even tried to drown him, but he was saved by sea nymphs. The latter version of the myth is most relevant to Wayland. In Germanic mythology the master craftsmen were mainly dwarfs, and Wayland's own mother was a mermaid. It is interesting to note that Lemnos was an island with volcanic activity, like the remote island to which Wayland had been banished.

WIELAND see *WAYLAND*

WODEN see *ODIN*

WOTAN see *ODIN*

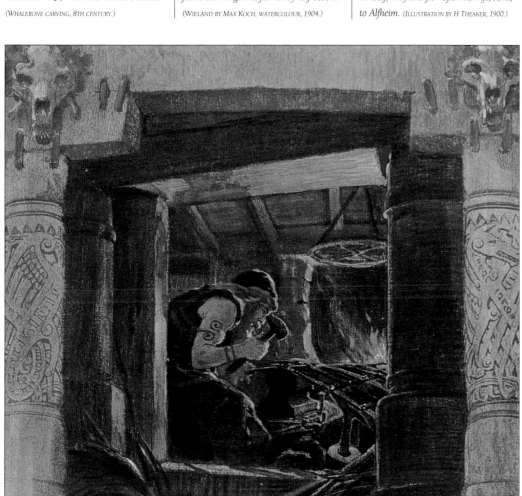

Y

YGGDRASIL, or Yggdrasill, (which means something like "dreadful mount") was the cosmic ash tree in Germanic mythology. Its name is a reference either to the gallows or *ODIN*'s horse. Not only did Odin hang himself on Yggdrasil for nine nights in order to learn wisdom, but sacrificial hangings from gallows trees were also a favourite Viking way of worshipping the god. An archaeological find that reveals the extent of this ghastly ritual is the Tollund Man, found in a Jutland peat bog in 1950. The corpse was so well preserved that it was possible to deduce that he was a prisoner of war who had been sacrificed as a thank-offering after a battle.

The parallel between Odin's voluntary death on Yggdrasil and

YGGDRASIL (right) the World Tree, lay at the heart of the universe. Here, the whirling patterns of Viking art strikingly capture the swirling vitality at the centre of life. A stag browses on its evergreen foliage while a serpent nips the stag's neck, reflecting the life and death struggle at the root of life.
(WOOD CARVING, 8TH CENTURY.)

YMIR (below) was the first creature to emerge from the primal wastes of ice in the yawning abyss of Ginnungagap at the dawn of creation. As fire from the south melted ice from the north, the icy droplets fused to form a massive frost giant. As he slept, his sweat formed other frost giants.
(ILLUSTRATION BY NICK BEALE, 1995.)

the Crucifixion remains striking. Odin was also pierced with a spear and, like Christ, cried out before he died. Although it is possible that the Crucifixion was known at the time that the Odin myth was recorded, there is little doubt that his hanging on the cosmic tree had pre-Christian origins and derived from ancient pagan worship. Odin had long been the god of the spear, the god of the hanged.

Yggdrasil is described as the largest and most stately tree ever to have grown. Its branches overhung the nine worlds and spread out above the heavens. It was supported by three great roots: one descended to *JOTUNHEIM*, the land of the giants, where *MIMIR*'s well stood; the second ended in foggy Niflheim, close by the spring of Hvergelmir, where the dragon *NIDHOGG* gnawed the root from below whenever it tired of chewing corpses; the last root was embedded near *ASGARD*, the stronghold of the gods, beneath *URD*'s well, where the gods held their daily assembly. Water was taken from the well each day by the *NORNS*, the three fates, Urd, Skuld and Verdandi, and mixed with earth as a means of preventing Yggdrasil's bark from rotting. An eagle perched on the very top of the cosmic tree

was daily harassed by a squirrel named Ratatosk, who brought unpleasant comments and insults up from the dragon Nidhogg. Another bird in its branches was a cock, sometimes referred to as "Vidofnir the tree snake".

The idea of a cosmic tree is common in the myths of the northern parts of both Europe and Asia. It was thought of as the backbone of the universe, the structural support of the nine worlds. In Ireland, however, the sacred tree acquired a different role. Although always associated with otherworld splendour, the musical branches of Irish mythology acted as cures for

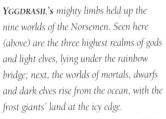

YGGDRASIL's mighty limbs held up the nine worlds of the Norsemen. Seen here (above) are the three highest realms of gods and light elves, lying under the rainbow bridge; next, the worlds of mortals, dwarfs and dark elves rise from the ocean, with the frost giants' land at the icy edge.

(ILLUSTRATION FROM NORTHERN ANTIQUITIES, 1847.)

YGGDRASIL (right) filled the known world, taking root not only in the dark depths of Niflheim (bottom), but also in Midgard and Asgard. Its topmost boughs reached heaven, while its lowest root touched hell. It was generally thought of as the structural support of the universe.

(ILLUSTRATION BY ALAN LEE, 1984.)

sickness and despair. In a number of tales these magic branches of silver or gold were brought by messengers from otherworld lands. Thus the fabulous voyage of Bran began with the sound of music that caused him to fall asleep. It came from a branch of silver with white blossoms, which a beautiful lady took away after telling of the delights of her world beyond the sea. Hints of such magic are also present in Germanic mythology. The obvious example must be the apples belonging to the goddess *IDUN*. Only this magic fruit prevented the gods from growing old. They were clearly the gift from

another sacred tree. How much trees were once revered can be seen from the reactions to early Christian missionaries like St Boniface. In the eighth century he cut down sacrificial trees, to the terror of the Frisians, until he himself was felled at Dockum by an outraged pagan.

YGGDRASILL see YGGDRASIL

YMIR, in Germanic mythology, was the first living creature. He was a frost giant who emerged from the ice in *GINNUNGAGAP* ("the yawning emptiness"). He was evil and the father and mother of all frost giants, who first came from the sweat of

his armpit. Ymir fed on the milk of the primeval cow *AUDHUMLA*. He was slain by the brothers *ODIN*, *VILI* and *VE*, who were the grandsons of *BURI*, whom Audhumla had licked free of the ice.

Growing tired of the brutality of Ymir and his ever-increasing band of frost giants, Odin, Vili and Ve took up arms. They slew Ymir and then drowned all the frost giants in his blood, with the exception of *BERGELMIR* and his wife, who managed to escape by sailing on a hollowed tree trunk.

Odin, Vili and Ve then threw Ymir's carcass into Ginnungagap. His flesh became the earth, his

unbroken bones mountains, his teeth and jaw rocks and boulders, his blood rivers, lakes and the sea, and his skull the sky, which was held up at its four corners by dwarfs. Sparks were used to make the sun, the moon and the stars.

Such an extremely violent creation myth is by no means unique. The Babylonian champion of the gods, Marduk, slew the chaos-dragon Tiamat with raging winds and an arrow, before splitting her carcass into two parts. One he pushed upwards to form the heavens, the other he used to make a floor above the deep, the emptiness at the bottom of the universe.

NORSE FAMILY TREES

ODIN

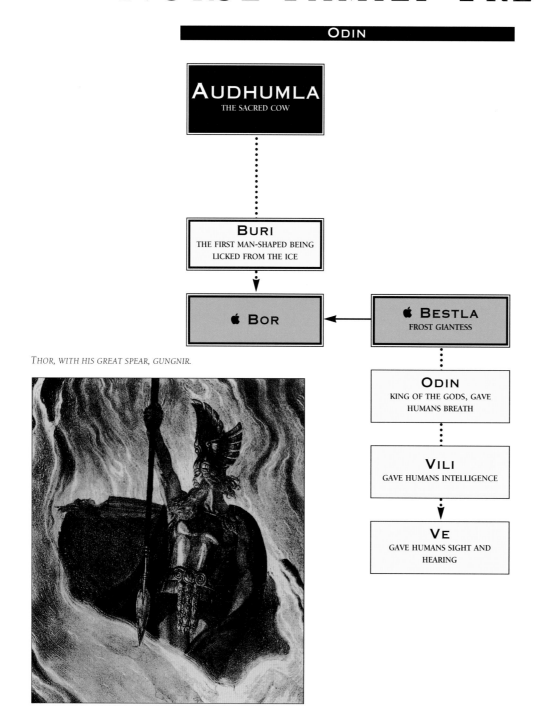

AUDHUMLA
THE SACRED COW

BURI
THE FIRST MAN-SHAPED BEING
LICKED FROM THE ICE

 BOR

 BESTLA
FROST GIANTESS

ODIN
KING OF THE GODS, GAVE
HUMANS BREATH

VILI
GAVE HUMANS INTELLIGENCE

VE
GAVE HUMANS SIGHT AND
HEARING

THOR, WITH HIS GREAT SPEAR, GUNGNIR.

EXPLANATORY NOTE

*The following family trees have been laid out to illustrate the
various unions and children between important gods and
goddesses described in this book. The sign denotes sexual
relationships (in and out of wedlock) and any dotted line
descending from the sign shows the child or children of that union.
Where one of the parents is unknown, the line descends straight
from the mother or father.*

As the leader of the gods, Odin could trace his
ancestry back in a straight line to the beginning
of the world, when the sacred cow Audhumla
and the frost giant Ymir were created by the meeting of
cold and flame. Then Audhumla licked Buri out of a
salty block of ice. Together with his two brothers, Odin
used Ymir's body to make the earth, the waters and the
skies. They also fashioned the first humans. Odin
himself was believed to have fathered all the other Aesir
gods (see the Aesir, opposite). His followers revered
him for his wisdom.

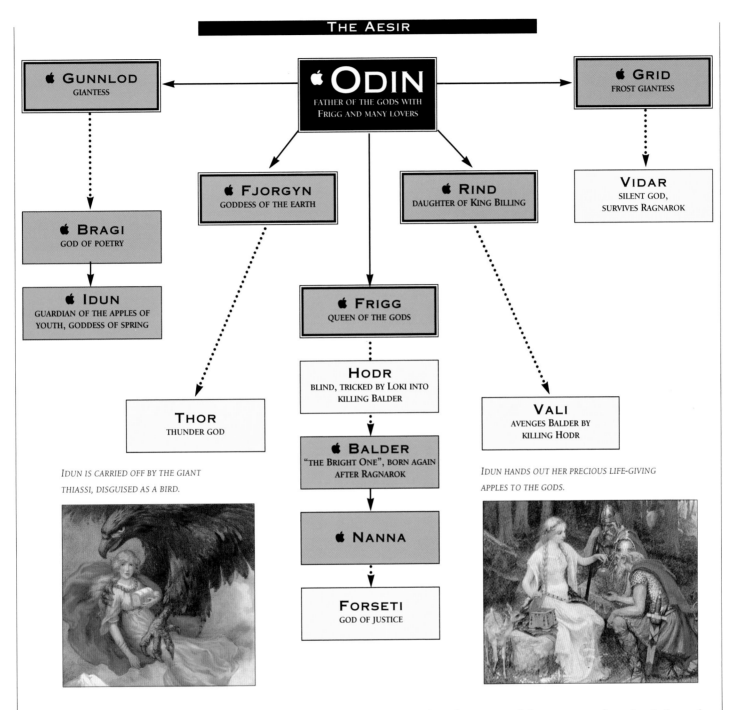

THE AESIR

GUNNLOD
GIANTESS

ODIN
FATHER OF THE GODS WITH
FRIGG AND MANY LOVERS

GRID
FROST GIANTESS

BRAGI
GOD OF POETRY

FJORGYN
GODDESS OF THE EARTH

RIND
DAUGHTER OF KING BILLING

VIDAR
SILENT GOD,
SURVIVES RAGNAROK

IDUN
GUARDIAN OF THE APPLES OF
YOUTH, GODDESS OF SPRING

FRIGG
QUEEN OF THE GODS

HODR
BLIND, TRICKED BY LOKI INTO
KILLING BALDER

THOR
THUNDER GOD

VALI
AVENGES BALDER BY
KILLING HODR

BALDER
"THE BRIGHT ONE", BORN AGAIN
AFTER RAGNAROK

*IDUN IS CARRIED OFF BY THE GIANT
THIASSI, DISGUISED AS A BIRD.*

*IDUN HANDS OUT HER PRECIOUS LIFE-GIVING
APPLES TO THE GODS.*

NANNA

FORSETI
GOD OF JUSTICE

The Aesir were the gods and goddesses led by Odin. Predominantly connected with warfare, they lived in Asgard, a mighty stronghold where the souls of the bravest men killed in battle were taken after death by the Valkyries. After settling an early conflict with the Vanir, another race of gods (see p.92), the Aesir turned their attention to fighting the frost giants. Despite their divinity, the Aesir were not immortal. Many of them were fated to die during Ragnarok, the doom of the gods, when Loki and his children united with the giants to attack Asgard.

Although Odin was widely recognized as the father of all gods, there were deities among the Aesir whose parentage was disputed. Tyr, for example, the war god who gave his name to Tuesday, was said by some to be the son of Odin, but by others to be the son of a giant named Humir. Heimdall, the watchman of the gods who stood guard on the rainbow bridge Bifrost, was the son of nine mothers and himself fathered children in the human world of Midgard. Furthermore, Odin's brothers Vili and Ve, while far less important, were counted among the Aesir.

THE CHILDREN OF LOKI

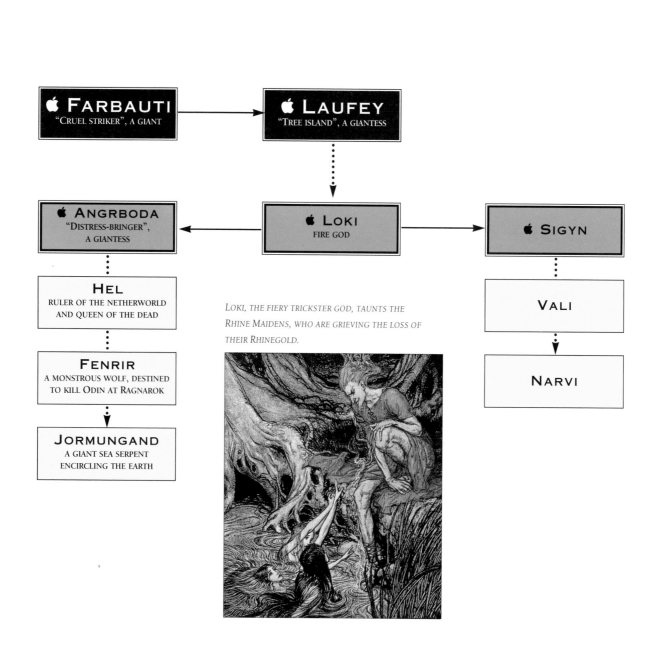

FARBAUTI
"CRUEL STRIKER", A GIANT

LAUFEY
"TREE ISLAND", A GIANTESS

ANGRBODA
"DISTRESS-BRINGER",
A GIANTESS

LOKI
FIRE GOD

SIGYN

HEL
RULER OF THE NETHERWORLD
AND QUEEN OF THE DEAD

FENRIR
A MONSTROUS WOLF, DESTINED
TO KILL ODIN AT RAGNAROK

JORMUNGAND
A GIANT SEA SERPENT
ENCIRCLING THE EARTH

VALI

NARVI

*LOKI, THE FIERY TRICKSTER GOD, TAUNTS THE
RHINE MAIDENS, WHO ARE GRIEVING THE LOSS OF
THEIR RHINEGOLD.*

Since his parents were giants, Loki was not strictly speaking one of the gods, but he lived with them in Asgard. A shape-shifter and a mischief-maker, he was tolerated until he brought about the death of Odin's son Balder, the personification of goodness. Then the gods turned on him and bound him, in an effort to contain the evil he had come to represent. But it was through Loki that the gods were fated to meet their doom, for at the end of the world he would be freed from his prison and join his monstrous children to fight the last battle of Ragnarok.

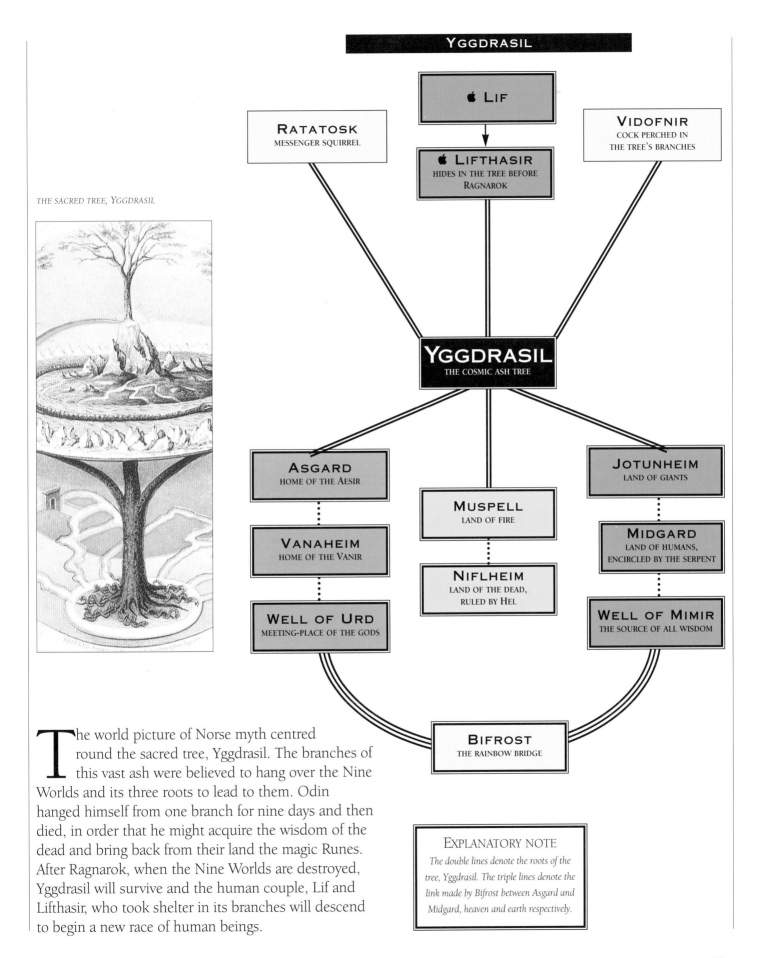

YGGDRASIL

LIF

LIFTHASIR
HIDES IN THE TREE BEFORE RAGNAROK

RATATOSK
MESSENGER SQUIRREL

VIDOFNIR
COCK PERCHED IN THE TREE'S BRANCHES

YGGDRASIL
THE COSMIC ASH TREE

THE SACRED TREE, YGGDRASIL

ASGARD
HOME OF THE AESIR

MUSPELL
LAND OF FIRE

JOTUNHEIM
LAND OF GIANTS

VANAHEIM
HOME OF THE VANIR

MIDGARD
LAND OF HUMANS, ENCIRCLED BY THE SERPENT

NIFLHEIM
LAND OF THE DEAD, RULED BY HEL

WELL OF URD
MEETING-PLACE OF THE GODS

WELL OF MIMIR
THE SOURCE OF ALL WISDOM

BIFROST
THE RAINBOW BRIDGE

The world picture of Norse myth centred round the sacred tree, Yggdrasil. The branches of this vast ash were believed to hang over the Nine Worlds and its three roots to lead to them. Odin hanged himself from one branch for nine days and then died, in order that he might acquire the wisdom of the dead and bring back from their land the magic Runes. After Ragnarok, when the Nine Worlds are destroyed, Yggdrasil will survive and the human couple, Lif and Lifthasir, who took shelter in its branches will descend to begin a new race of human beings.

EXPLANATORY NOTE

The double lines denote the roots of the tree, Yggdrasil. The triple lines denote the link made by Bifrost between Asgard and Midgard, heaven and earth respectively.

THE FAMILY OF SIGURD

HREIDMAR
ACQUIRES GOLD FROM LOKI
BUT IS KILLED FOR IT BY
FAFNIR AND REGIN

VOLSUNG
A MIGHTY WARRIOR

OTTER
KILLED BY LOKI

SIGMUND
OWNER OF A MAGIC SWORD

HJORDIS
(IN GERMAN SIEGLINDE)

FAFNIR
BECOMES A DRAGON
TO GUARD THE GOLD

REGIN
FOSTER FATHER TO SIGURD

GUDRUN
(IN GERMAN GUNNER)

SIGURD
KILLS FAFNIR TO OBTAIN
THE GOLD

GRIMHILD OFFERS AN UNSUSPECTING SIGURD HER MAGIC MEAD.

The story of the young hero Sigurd (known by the Germans as Siegfried) belongs as much to heroic legend as to myth, though it is connected with the Norse gods through the part played in the tale by Loki and through Sigmund's magic sword, thrust into a tree by Odin. As in many folk traditions, the possession of fabulous treasure brings disaster to the man who acquires it. Even Sigurd, otherwise an innocent figure, is fated to lose Brynhild, the beautiful Valkyrie whom he loves, when he is bewitched into marrying Gudrun.

THOR

| **⚫ ODIN** | → | **⚫ FJORGYN** |
| KING OF ALL THE AESIR GODS | | ALSO KNOWN AS JORTH, GODDESS OF THE EARTH |

| **⚫ SIF** | ← | **⚫ THOR** | → | **⚫ JARNSAXA** |
| GODDESS OF THE HARVEST, THOR'S WIFE | | GOD OF THUNDER, GAVE HIS NAME TO THURSDAY | | GIANTESS, THOR'S MISTRESS |

MAGNI
STRONG FROM BIRTH

MODI
DESTINED WITH MAGNI TO SURVIVE RAGNAROK

THOR, CHAMPION OF THE GODS.

O ne of the most popular of the Aesir, Thor was renowned as a great warrior. He was enormous, even for a god, and his strength and courage made him a formidable enemy of the giants in many adventures. Although his simple-mindedness laid him open to mockery from the other gods, it endeared him to the ordinary farmers who worshipped him throughout Scandinavia. Thor's chief weapon was Mjollnir, his magic hammer, which created thunder when he flung it down on the earth. The vast hall in Asgard where he lived with Sif was called Bilskirnir, or Lighting.

THE VANIR

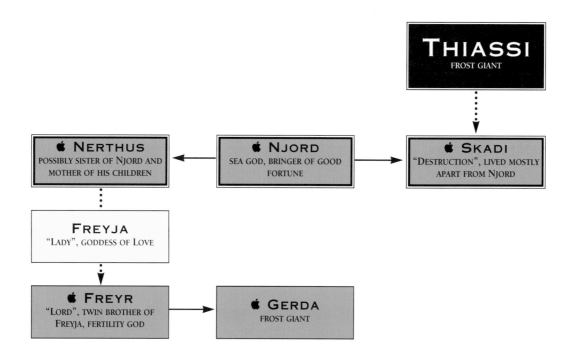

THIASSI
FROST GIANT

 NERTHUS
POSSIBLY SISTER OF NJORD AND
MOTHER OF HIS CHILDREN

 NJORD
SEA GOD, BRINGER OF GOOD
FORTUNE

 SKADI
"DESTRUCTION", LIVED MOSTLY
APART FROM NJORD

FREYJA
"LADY", GODDESS OF LOVE

 FREYR
"LORD", TWIN BROTHER OF
FREYJA, FERTILITY GOD

 GERDA
FROST GIANT

*FREYJA WAS RENOWNED FOR HER MAGICAL CRAFTS,
ALONG WITH THE OTHER VANIR DEITIES OF FERTILITY
AND NATURE.*

Unlike the warlike Aesir, the Vanir were a race of gods associated with fertility, with wealth and with good weather. They were believed by some to have existed before the Aesir and lived in their own world of Vanaheim. At first the two divine races were hostile to each other and conflict broke out between them. They eventually agreed to live in peace with each other, but the Vanir faded in significance. The best-known of their number were Freyr and Freyja, twins endowed with magical powers, who went to live in the Aesir's home of Asgard.

INDEX

V

W

Y

Z

PICTURE ACKNOWLEDGEMENTS

The Publishers gratefully acknowledge the following for permission to reproduce the illustrations indicated.

Ateneum, Helsinki, The Central Art Archives: 31BL, 37T, 54R, 55TL, 55TR, 75B.

Archiv fur Kunst und Geschichte, London: 13R, 15BR, 22BL, 24B, 31BR, 40TL, 40BR, 49B, 63TR, 68, 71TL, 71BL, 76TL, 76BR, 77T, 79ML, 80B, 83B.

Arnamagnaean Institute, Copenhagen: 10L, 36BL, 37BR.

Bildarchiv Preussisher Kulturbesitz: 58T.

The Bridgeman Art Library/Bonhams: 13L/Royal Library, Copenhagen: 32BR, 35 (both).

Jean Loup Charmet: 31TR, 58B.

Christies Images: 46T, 63BR.

E. T. Archive: 20T, 47B.

Fine Art Photographic Library: 22T, 77BR.

Alan Lee: 15T, 17T, 18ML, 28T, 29B, 39T, 56TR, 70BL, 71TR, 74, 79MR, 85TR.

Nasjonalgalleriet, Oslo: 20B, 48B.

National Museum Stockholm: 6-7, 16T, 24T, 49T, 64BL.

Statens Museum fur Kunst, Copenhagen: 15BL, 33T, 79TR, 82B.

Werner Forman Archive: 8, 44BL, 84TR/National Musuem, Copenhagen: 70BR/Statens Historiska Museum, Stockholm: 23TL, 31TL, 39BR, 43BL, 47TR, 79TL/Thjodminjasafin, Reykjavik: 67TL/Universitetets Oldsaksamling, Oslo: 9.

B = bottom, T = top, M = middle, L = left, R = right